Hearing the
Voice of God

Hearing the
Voice of God

A Practical Guide

Brian Neil Peterson

RESOURCE *Publications* · Eugene, Oregon

HEARING THE VOICE OF GOD
A Practical Guide

Copyright © 2018 Brian Neil Peterson. All rights reserved. Except for brief quotations in critical publications or reviews, no part of this book may be reproduced in any manner without prior written permission from the publisher. Write: Permissions, Wipf and Stock Publishers, 199 W. 8th Ave., Suite 3, Eugene, OR 97401.

Resource Publications
An Imprint of Wipf and Stock Publishers
199 W. 8th Ave., Suite 3
Eugene, OR 97401

www.wipfandstock.com

PAPERBACK ISBN: 978-1-5326-5530-2
HARDCOVER ISBN: 978-1-5326-5531-9
EBOOK ISBN: 978-1-5326-5532-6

Manufactured in the U.S.A. 07/16/18

This book is dedicated to my third child (my second son), Kevin. You are a part of God's greater plan for my life. Long before you were born, my wife and I prayed for you and asked for your safe delivery and God's blessings on your life. You are the visible results of answered prayer. As such, you are indeed a part of what it means to "hear the voice of God" in a tangible way. May God watch over you as you grow, and may you, too, learn to hear the voice of God for yourself as you mature in Him.

Contents

Preface | ix

Acknowledgments | xi

1. Introduction | 1
2. Hearing the Voice of God | 5
3. God Speaks through His Word | 14
4. God Speaks through the Prophetic Voice | 19
5. God Speaks through Others | 25
6. God Speaks to Confirm Your Calling | 30
7. God Speaks through Dreams and Visions | 38
8. God Speaks through the Moving and Prompting of the Spirit | 45
9. God Speaks through Events | 52
10. God Speaks through Signs | 60
11. God Speaks through a Still Small Voice | 65
12. God Speaks through Answered Prayer | 72
13. God Speaks through the Silence of Unanswered Prayer | 77
14. God Speaks through His Miraculous Protection | 87
15. God Speaks through His Acts of Healing | 95
16. Conclusion | 102

Preface

WHAT DOES HEARING THE voice of God actually look like? Does it entail hearing a voice from heaven? Is it only hearing God speak through his Word or through nature? Is God's voice heard clearest through a prophetic utterance, a word of knowledge, a dream, a vision, or a message in tongues with an interpretation? How do you know you are hearing the voice of God? In fact, does God still speak to believers today, or was that only for biblical times? These and similar questions are frequently asked by students when they come to my office for advice related to ascertaining God's direction in their lives. If we are honest, most Christians I am sure would love to have Jesus sitting across the table from them so they could talk with him for five minutes. If that happened then we could get clear direction for our future, such as, the degree we should take, the job we should apply for, the spouse we should marry etc., etc., etc. Most times this desire to hear God speak can be boiled down to the simple query: "What does God desire for me to do in this particular situation?"

    I would like to be able to tell people that there is a simple easy formula for hearing God's voice, but then, I would not be giving the whole picture. Hearing the voice of God takes practice. Moreover, God does not always speak in the way we expect. As a matter of fact, I have been learning my entire lifetime about what this looks like and how God speaks in the midst of a variety of situations. I have written this book in light of the questions noted

Preface

above and in response to the fundamental desire of my Christian students to know how and when God speaks.

Today, most people appreciate transparency and authenticity. They desire for others to be "real" with them. As such, I have attempted to write this book from this perspective. In other words, this book is deeply personal. In the chapters that follow, I have addressed a number of ways I have heard God's voice when seeking his direction and while simply living life one day at a time as a believer. Many of the specific accounts in this book were included based upon questions—like those noted above—that I have been asked by my students over the past several years. I must warn my reader, however, that this book is not your typical "how to" book dealing with prayer and hearing the voice of God. What I have done here is to show *how* God actually has spoken to me through a variety of personal experiences. By doing this the reader can gain an understanding of what hearing the voice of God actually looks like in real life. What is more, I have rooted these experiences in biblical precedent. I am not attempting to offer my reader some newfangled way of hearing God's voice; on the contrary, many of these ways of hearing God's voice are as old as time.

My ultimate goal for writing this book is to share with my reader how I communicate with God and hear his voice in order to help believers, young and old, to succeed in hearing God's voice for themselves. At the same time, even though this book may be geared to a younger audience, its message is not only for them. Anyone wanting an easy read on what hearing the voice of God looks like in very practical ways will hopefully enjoy their journey through my past forty-five plus years of living with God and learning how he speaks in the midst of daily life.

Acknowledgments

I would like to express my gratitude and thanks to my wife, Christine, for helping me edit and make the final manuscript more readable. I would also like to thank my freshmen classes from the spring of 2018 at Lee University for giving me feedback on the opening preface of this book.

Chapter 1

Introduction

I HAVE NEVER FORGOTTEN a sermon I heard by a guest speaker during my undergraduate degree at Zion Bible Institute, a small Bible school in Barrington, Rhode Island. In the sermon the speaker gave an illustration for his discussion by setting three chairs on the platform. He noted that each chair represented a generation of Christian people. The first chair represented the person who experienced salvation as the first of his/her family. The second chair represented the children of that first person, that is, the second "generation." Those in this second generation witnessed firsthand the glorious movement of God's Spirit in the lives of their parent(s) and tried to model that experience. The third chair in turn represented the grandchildren of the first person. These people either did not personally witness what their grandparent(s) and parent(s) had experienced concerning the power of the Spirit or they had simply taken it for granted. As such, this group tended to become cool towards the things of God. By extension, many in the fourth generation in this lineage had moved completely away from God and in no way lived according to godly principles. The point the preacher was making was clear: something happened in the passing on of one's spiritual heritage throughout the generations that allowed a "break in the chain" to occur as it relates to trusting in God.

As a third generation Pentecostal, I was deeply troubled by what this sermon illustration meant for me. Thankfully, my mom and grandparents set an example that has translated into the reality that many in my generation (represented by the third chair) still love and serve God faithfully. At the same time, sadly, many of the fourth generation in my family, due to a variety of factors, do not serve God. As a father of four children, I do not want my children, who represent the fourth generation, to falter in carrying forward the experience of their great grandparents, their grandparents, and their parents. I want them to know how to have a meaningful relationship with their God (cf. Judg 2:10). Of course, the key part of having a relationship with God is knowing how he speaks to his children. This is one of the reasons that I decided to write this book. The second reason is my desire to help others, my students in particular, to know how God can and does speak today.

"But What Does He Know?"

Perhaps some might say that I should have waited until I am much older to write a book like this, after all, I do not even have grandchildren yet. While it is true that I pray that God will continue to speak to me as I age and grow in him, it is also true that in our increasingly skeptical and God-rejecting day and age people need to hear about the goodness of God and how God actually still speaks to Christians *throughout* their lives. As opposed to waiting to offer reflections on an earlier life, long since passed, I wanted to share my past and ongoing experiences. In fact, the vibrant Christian life should exhibit a continuous litany of experiences of not only speaking with God, but hearing from him as well. As I enter my midlife I feel God has given me something to say in this regard.

In this vein, I want my children and my students to know what it looks like for God to speak with *his* children. God makes it clear that it is incumbent upon parents and grandparents to pass on the good things that God has done for them. Indeed, Israel is instructed to teach their children while sitting in their houses, walking along the road, and when they rise up and lay down (Deut

Introduction

6:7; 11:19). Even though this instruction focused on the teaching of the Law, it also included teaching the next generation (Deut 4:9) about the goodness of God and how he speaks to those who are his followers.

This book is not meant to be only autobiographical—focusing on my personal encounters with a God who communicates with his children—but it is also meant to be instructional on how to hear the voice of God based upon biblical principles and biblical precedents. The experiences I have had with God over the past four decades have shaped my faith and my trust in him. At the same time I want to make it clear to my readers that I am not trying to present myself as the "perfect" Christian. God forbid! I have found that God has spoken to me in the midst of my failures and when I least expect it. Part of maturing in my faith has been learning how my heavenly Father not only speaks to me, but also forgives me and picks me up when I fall. The recording of these accounts is also my way of acknowledging that God has been with me from my earliest days; even before he formed me in my mother's womb (Jer 1:5).

One of my earliest recollections of my childhood is me lying on the grass beside my mom's garden as she worked planting her vegetables. I was looking up into the vastness of the sky wondering what my purpose in life was. Even at that early stage in life I longed for God to show me his plan for my life. I desired for him to speak to me. I know that God heard that innocent prayer and saw my desire because from a very young age I have always had a sense of God's presence and working in my life. As I got older I began to recognize *how* God was actually speaking to me through a variety of means.

At the same time, and in light of my own journey, I can appreciate why many individuals, younger people in particular, would wonder how God speaks to the believer. Indeed, how does an infinite Being communicate to a lowly human? Not surprisingly, the psalmist struggled with this very concept when he wrote, "What is a person that you would take thought of them? And humans that you would care for them?" (Ps 8:4; my translation). As noted in the

Preface above, does God speak to us audibly as he did with Moses? Does he communicate through dreams and visions as experienced by the prophets? Does he use other people, events and/or circumstances in our lives, nature, or signs? What about prophetic utterances, glossolalia, words of knowledge or discernment? Are any, or all, of these modes of communication how God speaks to lowly humanity today? Or does he only speak through the Incarnation (Phil 2:5–10)?

The truth is God can speak through all of these methods and many others. To be sure, God has used a variety of ways to speak to me throughout my life. However, before beginning my discussion of how specifically God has worked in my life, I would like to examine how you can identify *when* God is actually speaking to you as opposed to hearing your own voice or the voice of the Enemy.

Chapter 2

Hearing the Voice of God

How Does One Discern God's Voice?

ONE OF THE MOST frequently asked questions by my students is how I discern the voice of God when making life decisions. This certainly is not an easy question to answer especially when you are learning how to discern the voice of God for yourself. In such cases, I am reminded of the clear biblical example of Samuel as a boy. One night while Samuel was sleeping he heard the voice of God simply calling his name: "Samuel" (1 Sam 3:4, 6, 8, 10). Of interest in this account is the fact that the Bible makes it clear that Samuel had not yet learned to discern the voice of God (1 Sam 3:7). The truth is, many Christians, especially those who have recently come to the faith or who are younger in age, have not yet learned how God speaks to them. This is not to slight anyone's experience with God but rather to encourage them to listen closely and to know that like any relationship, time strengthens it and allows you to recognize God's voice. Moreover, people need to appreciate the fact that God is not a God of coincidences. As a believer, I rarely chalk up the God-inspired experiences in my life to mere coincidence. As followers of Jesus we need to recognize that if God is with us at all times, and if he hears us, then the events of our lives should in fact reflect that reality. In other words, we should expect God to speak to us.

It really is quite exhilarating when one stops and considers that the God of the universe actually takes the time to speak with each of his children in unique and special ways. As a father of four I can truly appreciate this reality. I have a unique relationship with each of my children. My daughter Maddie knows how to get my attention: she knows how to ask her daddy for the things she wants. For instance, she loves to come and ask me to make for her one of my homemade "meat" sandwiches. That is her way of asking for a roast beef, chicken, or ham sandwich with mayo, mustard, and a bit of pepper. Another one of my favorites is when she comes to me in the morning, or before I go to bed, and whispers in my ear, "Daddy can just you and me go to McDonalds for breakfast?" She longs for father-daughter time without her two brothers in tow. My middle child, Mark, loves to ask for one-on-one time at the office with his dad where he can watch his favorite kids' shows on the computer and perhaps go through the drive-thru for ice cream on our way home. He also frequently asks for me to take him for a ride on his bike around our neighborhood. My youngest son, Kevin, just loves to run to greet his dad when I get home and spend time with me as I relax for a few minutes after work. He is also the only child who eats almost every meal on my lap, eating from his daddy's plate. Of course, this latter experience has its own challenges, especially when one of us is sick. My fourth child, Evelyn, was just born this summer so I await to see what specific connections she will have with me.

The point of commonality in my experiences with my children is one of personalized intimacy. Through this process, each of my kids individually is learning what my *character* is like by spending time with me. Moreover, as my children grow they learn how to trust and depend on me. They are learning that when I say something, I will follow through. This is a process and does not happen overnight. For example, when I drop my kids off at the nursery at church, they all had to learn that daddy or mommy will be back to pick them up. The key comparison I want to point out between how I and my children interact, and how God speaks to us as believers, is the common desire of each to get to know the other. This is done by spending time together. Like me and my children, believers learn what God's character is like over time. In essence, discerning the voice of God comes from spending time with our heavenly Father and learning about his character and how he acts, that is, how he speaks to us. In this process of learning, we also learn that we can depend on him.

Whose Voice Is Speaking To You?

The relationship I have with my children allows us to know each other's voice and to foster a relationship. In the same way I know and recognize each of my children's voices, so, too, they know the difference between my voice and that of my wife's, or anyone else's for that matter. As just noted with the early life of Samuel, Samuel did not know the difference between the voice of God and the voice of Eli. When students ask me how to discern the voice of God I point out that there are three "voices" between which one has to be able to differentiate: God's, our own, and Satan's. I will examine each of these in turn.

1. Knowing the Voice of God

It is this first Voice that is all-important to recognize. Jesus said, "My sheep hear My voice, and I know them, and they follow Me" (John 10:27; NASB). Of course, how does one go about hearing God's voice? This is the very point of this book. Because the remaining chapters of this book will give numerous examples of how I have personally come to recognize the voice of God, here I will only give some points of summary. First, when God speaks with us he will never contradict his written Word. If you feel God is telling you to do something that is clearly contradictory to his expressed Word (the Bible) then you can be assured it is either your voice or, more likely, the voice of the Enemy. A good example of how this plays out in everyday life is in the area of dating, especially when a believer tries to justify being romantically involved with an unbeliever. Due to the nature of the topic, this is a situation that is most often experienced by believers when they are younger; although older people who are single certainly are not exempt from this temptation.

When I teach the book of Hosea to my freshmen-level classes I discuss the life of Hosea and his "dating" relationship. I am quick to point out that Hosea was a unique case where a prophet is told by God to marry a prostitute, that is, an unbeliever (although she no doubt was a covenanted Israelite; Hos 1:2–3). This unique case does not give a believer the right to date or marry an unsaved individual. God's Word is replete with clear teaching against such actions (1 Cor 7:39; 2 Cor 6:14; cf. Exod 34:15; Deut 7:3; Josh 23:12; Ezra 9–10; Neh 13:23–28 etc.). Hosea was an inspired prophet whose very life became an example for all Israel. His life became a living hell as he watched his wife cheat on him time and again, a similar situation that Yahweh experienced with unfaithful Israel (Ezekiel 16; 23; Jeremiah 3). Apart from this one account, there is no case in the Bible where God *explicitly* tells someone to marry a pagan/unbeliever (Esther may appear to be an exception to the rule, but even here the Bible makes no mention of the fact that God told Esther to marry the Persian king.). As such, in this and similar cases, believers must always keep in mind that when God speaks, he never contradicts himself. He will always lead you in the way of truth as delivered through his inspired writers of the Bible.

The second thing to remember is that God's voice and word to you will always lead you to grow in him and give him glory. As I noted above when speaking about my experiences with my children, when God speaks to us it is for the purpose of learning how to trust in him and his guidance. The more I see God at work in my life the more I trust in him, love him, and praise him for who he is.

Third, we need to allow others to speak words of confirmation concerning what God is saying to us (see more in chapter 5). Sometimes—although not always—this tends to be very practical advice and guidance especially when you are dealing with big decisions like marriage, a career choice, or something else of high importance.

Finally, personally, I have found that God not only speaks to me when I least expect it, but when I need it the most. When I am experiencing a down moment or I am questioning his plans for my life it is in those moments God speaks to me through another person, a dream, an experience, the Bible, or perhaps even by his still small voice! When God speaks to us, many times it is to give us clear direction or at least point us to the right path. In moments like this, God's peace will follow.

2. When Am I Hearing My Voice?

I will say that from personal experience distinguishing between my voice/desires and the voice of God is very difficult. Because it is *our* life that we are dealing with, everything becomes personal, and in some cases, all-engrossing. As such, we must constantly check and recheck what we feel we are hearing from God. I know that on more than one occasion I have desired something so strongly that I have drowned out or clouded God's voice with my own. In those moments I have found myself in predicaments that were of my own making and once again in need of God's rescue. As I look back now on those moments in my life when I prayed so hard for something in particular and God had said "No," or "Wait," I cannot help but hear the words of that famous country song by Garth Brooks "Thank God for Unanswered Prayers!" God's plan is so much better than ours.

In all truthfulness, there is really no magic spiritual potion or silver bullet to use when trying to distinguish clearly between God's voice and our own. Experiencing God's voice over time is always the best solution to being able to distinguish his voice from ours. In some situations, what you want or desire may in fact be in line with God's plan. Indeed, in some cases, the Enemy may actually attempt to cause you to second guess what God is saying to you and what he has placed in your heart. But extreme caution is also in order because the Bible makes it clear that the heart is deceitful and wicked above all else and no one can truly know it (Jer 17:9). The best way to learn how to discern between the voice of God and your own is learning through experience and praying to God for clear direction and confirmation. In this vein, I have found that seeking confirmation from a secondary source (e.g., some other person, a dream, a prophetic word etc.) concerning what I have been praying about, or what I think I have heard God say to me, is one of the best ways to discern God's voice and to be assured that he is speaking.

3. Rejecting the Voice of Satan

When one truly knows the voice of God, recognizing the voice of the Enemy is often very easy. The Enemy will never tell you to do something that is going to make you a stronger believer. If anything, he sows seeds of doubt, which will drain you of certainty and hope. Furthermore, the Enemy will most certainly twist the Scriptures to try and convince the believer that what he is saying is correct. One needs to look no further than the experience of Jesus with Satan in the wilderness to realize this reality (Matt 4:1–10; Mark 1:13; Luke 4:1–12). Satan actually quoted Scripture to Jesus! He wanted Jesus to cast himself off the pinnacle of the temple because after all, God would protect him in such cases, right? (Ps 91:11). The problem was that Satan took the psalmist out of context. The psalmist was speaking of an unexpected encounter with danger, not an intentional testing of God's protective hand. Satan will never use the Bible correctly when he is tempting you to listen to him. It is also true that if you are not attuned to the voice of God that you can be led astray by the voice of Satan. Again, in most cases the Enemy will want you to do something against the clear teaching of Scripture/God. Satan's temptation of Eve is a fine example of this reality (Gen 3:1). At other times, Satan will tell you to do something purely for personal gain or pleasure. In the New Testament, James recognized this scenario and warned believers against it (James 1:13–15; 4:3). When a person listens to Satan the result will always be guilt and condemnation, never one of conviction: the Holy Spirit convicts, Satan condemns! Thus, one can conclude that the Bible is correct when it says that the Enemy goes about like a roaring lion seeking whom he may devour (1 Pet 5:8).

Hearing God through Others

Some may object to my categorization of the three main "voices" and suggest that there are other voices to consider: the voice of our friends and family, or perhaps the voice of our spiritual leaders. These voices are indeed part of our everyday lives but in essence can be placed into one of the three categories I first listed. God can, and does, use the voice of others (family, friends, and spiritual leaders) to reveal his will and to speak to us. And conversely, the Enemy can use these same voices to muddy the spiritual waters of our life. It is also possible that these same voices may tell us exactly what we want to hear without really taking into consideration the will of God.

Allow me to offer a few biblical examples to prove my point. In 2 Samuel 7, David, God's chosen king for the united kingdom of Israel, sought to build a temple/house for his God, Yahweh. Nathan, Yahweh's prophet, told David to go ahead, that God was with him in this endeavor. The problem was Nathan was reacting to David's desires without really considering what God wanted. That night Yahweh revealed to Nathan that David was not the one to build him a house; it would be a son of David who would build the temple. In this situation the very prophet of God had delivered a message to David that was not God's will. Fortunately, Nathan was spiritually alert enough to hear God speak clearly and rectify his error from the previous day. A second situation is more troubling. In the Old Testament false prophets would often tell a king exactly what they wanted to hear. Ahab's experience with his 400 false prophets and with the true prophet of Yahweh, Micaiah, certainly is exemplary of this type of situation (1 Kings 22). When the false prophets told Ahab what he wanted to hear (22:6, 11–12), Jehoshaphat, the godly king of Judah who was with Ahab, sought another word from God for confirmation (22:7). At this point Micaiah was called to confirm the word of the prophets of Ahab. Micaiah, being warned by Ahab's servant to deliver a confirming word, did just that (22:13–15). However, Ahab knew that Micaiah was not giving him the full message of God. How did God warn Micaiah of Ahab's demise? God gave him a vision of the death of Ahab (22:17–23; cf. 22:34–35). One could also point out the similar experience of Jeremiah with the false prophet Hananiah. In this situation, Jeremiah warned the people of the coming judgment of God on Zedekiah and Jerusalem while the false prophet Hananiah told the king exactly what he wanted to hear: God would deliver Jerusalem and bring the exiles home within two years (Jer 28:1–4, 10–11). Of course we know from history that Jeremiah was correct. God spoke to him through the prophetic word (Jer 28:5–9, 12–16). From a more positive perspective, God used the prophet Agabus in Acts to warn of Paul's difficulties in Jerusalem before Paul ventured there (Acts 21:10–11).

From these few examples it is clear that God can use friends and spiritual leaders to deliver a word from the Lord. In Pentecostal and charismatic circles, this can take on the form of tongues and interpretation, words of knowledge and discernment and even prophecy (1 Cor 12:7–10; see more below). However, I have also shown that based upon these biblical cases, one needs to test the words of others to make sure they are in fact from God (1 John 4:1–3). People can be sincere in their pronouncements but also be sincerely wrong. When my best friend Sandie was diagnosed with terminal ovarian cancer, more than one well-intentioned "prophet" of God told her she would recover. Unfortunately these "prophecies" did not come to fruition. How did a "prophet" get this so wrong? It is very possible that they, like Nathan the prophet with David, wanted to believe that God was with my friend and would in fact do what she desired. It is also possible that the Enemy was using these people to sow false hope and bring reproach to the name of God causing others to lose faith. The point is that in light of these types of unfortunate occurrences one must always be careful when discerning the voice of God through others. As

Hearing the Voice of God

I noted earlier and will develop more below, generally God uses other people to confirm the word of God already spoken to you in other ways. Even then, care must be taken to make sure this is God speaking. I have found that when I am making major life decisions, God will use a number of different means to confirm his word.

Although these examples and warnings may sound discouraging, I want to make it clear that there still is genuine communication between God and his creation. That is why in this book I will demonstrate to my readers through numerous personal experiences that God does speak to us; however, sometimes this may not be with the answers we want to hear. Indeed, God's silence can in fact be the answer we may need. God's silence may mean "no," or maybe, "not yet." My life has been full of God speaking to me through silence and waiting on him. At other times, however, God has given me direction in ways I can only say is nothing short of miraculous. It is also noteworthy that throughout my spiritual walk God has chosen to speak to me through a variety of means: dreams, God-ordained events, prophetic utterances, the prompting of the Spirit, and on at least one occasion, the audible voice of God. It is to these events of my life that I now turn in an effort to offer my reader hope and instruction when discerning the voice of God.

Chapter 3

God Speaks through His Word

ONE SHOULD NOT BE surprised that God can, and does, speak to people primarily through his written Word, that is, the Bible. As the recorded sacred word of God written by inspired authors (Rom 15:4; 2 Tim 3:16; 2 Pet 1:20–21), God puts his Word on par with even his own name (Ps 138:2). Daniel allowed the words of the prophet Jeremiah to speak to him during his day and age and considered what God was saying through this prophetic word to be vital to his present situation (Dan 9:2). And Micah appears to have cited Isaiah when delivering words of hope to his audience (cf. Micah 4:1–4; Isa 2:2–4). What is more, the biblical writers' use of the words of Moses are too numerous to list. Throughout the New Testament, the biblical writers appealed to the written words of the Hebrew and Greek versions of their Bible to speak into their present situations. Paul referenced not only the specific laws of Moses, but Genesis as well (Galatians 4; note also the actions of the Bereans in Acts 17:11), and Peter referred to the teachings of Paul as instructive (2 Pet 3:15–16). The author of Hebrews appealed to Leviticus, the author of John's gospel alluded to Ezekiel and quoted Isaiah, and John the Revelator loved to cite both Daniel and Ezekiel.

In light of the propensity of the biblical authors to rely on the written Word to speak to them, how much more so should believers go to the Bible to hear the words of God today? Now that is not to say that we should treat the Bible like a magic book opening it wherever we want and reading a verse to find an answer. While God might allow someone to use this method on occasion, this is not the norm. God tends to speak to people through systematic reading and study of the Bible, while at other times he brings to remembrance a particular passage that we have committed to memory in order to speak to us. God has used both of these methods to speak to me.

Getting an Answer from God for Service

During my first semester of my undergraduate degree I was asked to be a part of a traveling music and drama group. The problem was that it was a commitment of not only weekends and breaks during the school year but also six weeks during the summer. As a carpenter, this was the time when I made enough money to pay for all my schooling and expenses for the year. With only about sixteen weeks to work during the summer, this ministry opportunity would limit me to just ten weeks. After doing some number crunching I realized that this really would not be feasible for me to do. Although the practical part of me wanted to say, no, I could not shake the fact that I felt God wanted me to accept the ministry opportunity. I decided to take some time to pray so I told the group leader I would give him my answer in a few days.

During this time, I served as a security guard as part of my work on the campus. My shift was from 4–8 AM on select days. Not being a morning person I found this shift difficult. Nevertheless, I regularly got up and did my rounds and then found myself back at the guardhouse reading or studying for my next quiz. During that time of discernment concerning my service to the travel team I just happened to be reading through the book of Philippians. While I had never made it a habit to look for an answer to a question from some random text, this time as I read through Philippians one verse jumped off the page. The text was, "But my

God shall supply all your need according to his riches in glory" (Phil 4:19; KJV).

In the quietness of the early morning (cf. Ps 63:1) I felt that God was using this verse to speak to me about my possible service to the music and drama team. I quickly noted that the verse did not say that God would supply all my "wants" but rather all my "needs." I was not one to make a decision on a whim but I never felt any surer about making a decision than I did at that moment. I contacted the team leader that day and told him I would serve with him on his team. I would like to say that serving the team as their driver, stage hand, and as a part-time actor was always easy. In fact it was hard work. And driving early in the morning and late at night when I was tired was rough at times. But God did use me to minister to inner-city children, to witness to the lost, to preach his Word, and to see souls saved. When I returned in the fall to register for classes, I had enough money to cover all my expenses. God had given me extra work during that summer, and with a lot of overtime, the ten weeks of work allowed me to meet all my financial obligations for the next year.

God Speaks through the Prompting of a Biblical Passage

The four years I spent at Zion Bible College in Barrington, RI, were marked by many good times and positive memories. However, for the first year or so I had hidden my carpentry talents because I did not want to get bogged down in the many construction projects that needed to be done on the campus. I had worked for years as a carpenter and continued to do so during my breaks and the summers. I was tired of working so hard at that occupation so when I first arrived on campus, I did not say anything about being a licensed carpenter. Instead I applied to be on security detail. Because I was larger, and apparently intimidating, they assigned me to the security team.

Over the first year or so as I walked around the campus on my security rounds everywhere I looked I saw the need of a good carpenter. I felt that God was prompting me not to hide my talents but rather to use them for his glory and to help out where I could. I needed to use the gifts that God had given me to serve (Rom 12:6–8). Shortly thereafter I left the security detail and joined the maintenance team. For the last two or more years of my time at Zion I fixed roofs, laid floors, built cabinets, and a host of other projects, including building a new pulpit and communion table for the chapel. Despite all I had done, when I left the campus as a graduate in 2001, everywhere I looked there still was work to be done. In fact, the school needed a major infusion of capital to cover an overhaul of the entire campus.

Over the next few years I felt God impressing upon my heart to pray for financial assistance for the school. Even though I had moved on to my master's level work, I continued to return to the campus to visit old friends and I also continued to pray. I could not get away from the Bible verse that God owns the cattle on a thousand hills (Ps 50:10). God seemed to be continually reminding me that I needed to pray from that perspective. God could easily "sell" some of those "cattle" and meet the need of my alma mater. I thought of the many wealthy Christians that God had given so much to and I asked God to send along the right people to help with the need. Now I am sure many other people were praying as well, but for me this verse stood out as the basis of my prayers.

In 2007, while I was doing my PhD work in Toronto, Canada, I heard the good news that God had done something even greater than what I could imagine. He prompted David Green, the owner of Hobby Lobby, to purchase an entirely different campus in Haverhill, MA, and then renovate it and give it to Zion! The old rundown campus in Barrington, which was in need of so much capital expenditure, could now be sold and the money used to improve the much nicer campus in Haverhill. God had gone above and beyond what most of us could ever imagine. Indeed, he owns the cattle on a thousand hills and he had prompted one of the wealthier "cattle owners" to take Zion (now Northpoint) under his wing and help it to thrive. Through the continual prompting by God to pray a simple Bible verse, God had used me as a part of a larger prayer movement to see the fortunes of my alma mater change.

When I visited the new campus in 2008 with my wife, the dean of the school gave us a tour. As I walked around the campus I marveled at the goodness of God. Were there things that needed improvement? Yes. But it was nothing like I had witnessed at the old campus. Everything that needed repaired was either scheduled to be done—and done properly—or could be done fairly easily. As a carpenter I felt a sense of hope for the school. I left the campus with a renewed appreciation that God does indeed answer prayer.

Conclusion

I am sure that others will attest to the fact the God's Word is alive and living and that God uses it daily to speak to his children. What I noted above were just a couple examples of the numerous times God has spoken to me through reading the Bible. Yet, there are still other times when I read and I pray and it feels like the heavens are as brass. What is one to do in these situations? What if you feel you are reading what you want to see into the Bible? It is at times like this that God can give very specific instruction through different avenues such as the prophetic office. Again, a word of warning is in order. God will never instruct you to do something contrary to his revealed, written Word. Christians must always submit their lives to Scripture as the final rule and authority.

Chapter 4

God Speaks through the Prophetic Voice

Perhaps one of the clearest ways of hearing from God is to have someone who is used in the prophetic office speak a word from the Lord into your life (1 Cor 12:28; Eph 4:11). Yet, as I noted earlier, believers must be cautious about the words spoken over them by prophetic voices, and be willing to test what modern prophets say to you (1 Cor 14:29). We have been forewarned that many false prophets are present among us (1 John 4:1). Indeed, the sign of the true prophet of God is whether his or her prophecy comes to pass (Deut 18:22). With this caveat I would add that the true prophet is one who speaks a word to you not having known what you have prayed and laid before God in the privacy of your prayer closet.

In this regard, I recall a time when my mom told me an account of how she had been reprimanded by a preacher for wanting to honor her parents concerning the way her children were baptized. My mom was deeply hurt and took her pain to God. A little later, while attending a special revival service, my mom was approached by an evangelist. He proceeded to speak a prophetic word over her addressing the very questions and hurts she had placed before God. In that moment, my mom knew that God was giving her direction through the voice of the prophet: she had never spoken a word to anyone about her inner turmoil but here a man of God had given her answers to the very questions she prayed in silence to God.

1. A Closed Book

Personally, three different times God has used someone gifted in the prophetic office to speak to me and give me direction. All three occurrences happened when I was about 28 years old. The first two times are very similar and happened only 24 hours apart. It was during a very formative part of my life when I was looking for God's direction on how to move forward after a series of setbacks in life. I did not realize at the time that this was the period when God was preparing me to make a change in my career and move me into my thirteen-year educational journey. The events unfolded as follows.

The pastor of our church at that time had arranged a series of revival meetings with a husband and wife evangelistic team. One night during these services, after all the musicians had finished playing for the altar service and we were around the altar basking in the Spirit's presence, one of the evangelists walked past the chair I was sitting in and then stopped and turned and looked at me. At that moment I had been in an attitude of prayer but I was not sure what was about to happen. I had been raised in Pentecostal circles all my life and so I was familiar with the prophetic voice/office. I was also somewhat skeptical of the often generic prophecies that traveling evangelists sometimes delivered to spiritually hungry parishioners. However, all that upbringing and skepticism had not prepared me for what the prophet of God spoke to me (I am paraphrasing the content of what was said). He asked me to get out of my seat and come to him. As I stood in front of him he looked me in the eye and said, "I see a book in front of you." He continued, "God is closing that book, which represents a part of your past life. He is saying, 'it is finished and over, now move on.'"

Much like had happened to my mom, only God knew what I had been praying about. Indeed, it was directly related to major changes taking place in my life. As my mind raced and quickly

God Speaks through the Prophetic Voice

reflected on what the evangelist had just spoken to me the Enemy reminded me that my past would always hold me back and that I would never amount to anything for God. As the exhilaration of hearing God's answer to this particularly important prayer began to be overshadowed by these stinging words of the Enemy the evangelist interrupted my thought process and continued his prophetic utterance. He continued, "Now I want you to look over your right shoulder." I thought he was being figurative, but he made it clear that he wanted me literally to look over my shoulder behind me. Not knowing exactly what the purpose for this spiritual exercise was, I followed his command—and yes, he was commanding me through the Spirit—and I looked over my right shoulder. Then the evangelist said, "Look as far back as you can"—in our small church it was the back wall. He then said, "Now, look over your left shoulder as far as you can." In obedience, and at the same time with trepidation, I looked over my left shoulder as far as I could see. My mind was racing. What could this exercise possibly mean? As I turned back to the evangelist and looked at him he said, "God wants you to know that everything behind you is in the past! God wants you to move forward. God has closed the book on your past and to him your past is gone." With these prophetic words, the accusations of the Enemy fell by the wayside. I was immediately released in the Spirit and I knew God had answered my prayers by means of this complete stranger. I wept before God in thankfulness for his words of deliverance and forgiveness. As I noted in chapter 1 above, you can tell the voice of God because it helps us to grow in God and it is redemptive.

    I left the service that night with a renewed faith that God was speaking to my circumstances and preparing me for any of the hardships that would unfold in my life. Like the woman taken in adultery in John 8, or the woman who washed Jesus' feet with her tears in Luke 7, God had wiped the sins of my past clean and was telling me to move forward. I would have been more than content to leave the prophetic word as it was delivered. After all, God had answered my private prayers in a way beyond what I could have ever imagined. But God is a loving and caring Father and knows our insecurities. God also knows and sees the beginning and the end of my life and so what happened next would only make sense later when I became a teacher of the Bible.

The very next night at the special services God again moved in a special way. Almost in a déjà vu fashion, after the preaching and singing during the altar service had pretty much come to a conclusion, I found myself sitting in almost the same seat as I had been the night before. As I sat there and began to reminisce about the previous night's blessing and prophetic word, the wife of the evangelist (who was also very much involved in her husband's evangelistic ministry) walked past me. She immediately stopped and turned around and looked at me. At first I thought she was merely going to exchange pleasantries. Boy was I wrong! She asked me to stand up and come and stand in front of her. You guessed it, she said, "I see a book in front of you." She continued, "I also see God closing that book, which represents a part of your past life. He is saying, 'it is finished and over, now move on.'" Of course, she went on to ask me to look over each shoulder as far as I could see and then she said, "God wants you to know that everything behind you is in the past! God wants you to move forward. God has closed the book on your past and to him your past is gone." You can well imagine how this struck me as strangely odd, but yet, encouraging. I know, some will say that the husband and wife colluded or that she had heard her husband the night before. The problem with that is that she had been nowhere near me and her husband the night before. She had been across the church in another part of the altar service. From my recollection, when her husband had spoken to me, he only spoke so I could hear. No one else did. While I thought this déjà vu moment odd at the moment, it would not be until later that this made perfect sense.

As I began my schooling a couple of years later I was surprised to find out that during my days in Sunday School I had missed some very important lessons on how God speaks to people and confirms his word. I learned that it was a common occurrence in the Bible for people to receive duplicates of dreams and prophetic words. When God wanted to make certain that people knew something was going to happen, he gave them duplicates of the prophetic or promised word. This happened to Joseph (Gen 37:6–10), Pharaoh (Gen 41:1–7), Samuel and Eli (1 Sam 2:27–36; 3:10–15), and others. God had used this husband and wife evangelistic duo to give to me these two identical prophetic words to confirm that he indeed knew where I was and that my past was in the past. These words would be a means of spiritual sustenance over the next few months as I faced some of the hardest moments in my life.

2. A Restored Life

From these two experiences I was beginning to learn how special I was to God. But God was not through with me yet when it came to speaking to me through the prophetic voice. On another occasion during this same period of my life another special speaker came to my home church. This speaker was unique in that he had been my camp counselor when I was eight or nine years old. I had not seen him for close to twenty years. He knew nothing about me other than the fact that as a camper I had been studious in memorizing Bible verses. One night as I sat in the front row of the church and the guest speaker was ministering, he stopped speaking and looked at me. A bit awkward and nervous I stared back at him. Out of the blue he said, "This guy knows Scripture frontwards and backwards. I can start a verse and he can finish it." Of course, that is exactly what he did and I finished the verse he was quoting. My time in camp and in AWANA had helped me hide God's word in my heart (Ps 119:11). Even though this was an interesting exchange, I was not sure what the purpose of it was, especially in front of everyone in the church. This quickly became clear, however, when the evangelist stopped speaking and walked over and laid his hand on my shoulder and said, "God is going to restore what the locusts and cankerworm has eaten." Immediately I knew this was a prophetic word coming directly from the Old Testament book of Joel, verse 2:25 to be exact.

Why was this so important? While I knew that God could wipe away my past and remove my sin and failures as far as the east is from the west (Ps 103:12), I was not sure if I could ever truly be happy again and experience restoration. In this moment God had used another prophetic word to confirm that as well. Again, this evangelist did not know what had transpired in those twenty years since I had seen him. Nor had he been "filled in" by others because he had just arrived at our church. What I find even more interesting is that a few years after this event during my first year of Bible school the drama and music team I had joined traveled throughout the eastern United States. On one of the times when we were on the road my team was billeted in a number of different homes for the night. I found myself in this same evangelist's home. I spoke to him and reminded him of what he had told me. From what I recall, he acknowledged that he spoke through the Spirit that night a few years earlier.

Conclusion

What do these three accounts teach us about how God speaks to his people? For one thing, we should never forsake the assembling of ourselves together (Heb 10:25). It is in the church that God many times uses others who are gifted in the prophetic office to speak to his people. We are part of a much larger body of believers and are not islands unto ourselves. It also taught me that even though some people have misused the gift of prophecy, God still uses it to give direction. I also recognized that in very important times in my life God could, and does, send his prophets and prophetesses to confirm his word, especially in those moments when the Enemy seeks to spread confusion.

Chapter 5

God Speaks through Others

SIMILAR TO HEARING GOD'S voice through the prophetic office, sometimes God can use people, Christians and non-Christians alike, to confirm God's working in our life and to let us know that he is with us. I have found that at key junctures in my life when I need clarity and direction God tends to cluster his signs and his workings. That is not to say that he is not with me at other times, but rather that God tends to give me reassurance at times when he is doing a new thing in my life. This is certainly the way we see God work within the Scriptures. The calling of men like Gideon and Saul are good examples. Gideon received a word from the angel of the Lord as well as God-given signs (Judges 6). Similarly, when Saul became king God used signs and others (Samuel and the people) to confirm his calling to be king (1 Samuel 9–12). Back in the 1990s God used a variety of means to get my attention in order to prove to me that he was with me. These types of events also prepared me for my time when I would study the Bible as a student and later when I would become a Bible professor.

1. God Speaks through Non-believers

Back in the 1990s and early 2000s I worked out regularly at my local gym. At that point in my life I had recently rededicated myself to Christ and I was finding my spiritual "legs." As such, I did not always wear my Christianity on my proverbial shirt sleeves for all to see. I often wondered how I could broach the topic of being a Christian with those I worked out with. During that time I became acquainted with a guy who lived in Houlton, Maine, and who frequented the gym where I worked out. Over a period of several weeks we crossed paths regularly and often spotted each other when we were lifting weights. Based upon his language and general demeanor, I could tell he was not a Christian. I had not said much about who I was other than the fact that I was a carpenter, played hockey, and liked to work out. One night as I was at the gym going through my regular workout routine, I met up with him. Out of the blue he stopped and looked at me and said, "Brian why are you different than everyone else here? I can tell something is different about you." Not only was I shocked, you could have knocked me over with a feather. God opened the door for me to share my faith with this gentleman. I cannot be certain what ever happened in the life of this guy, but through this experience God was telling me that he was working in my life even though up to this point I had said very little.

Rarely do I put much spiritual stock in the words of nonbelievers; however, there are numerous examples of God using unbelievers to confirm God's special calling of his people and to confirm that he is using them for his greater plans of ministering to others. For example, Elijah is first identified as the "prophet/man of God" not by an Israelite, but rather by an unbelieving Baal worshipping Phoenician woman (1 Kgs 17:24). Also, Jesus is identified as a prophet by the woman at the well (John 4:19); as sent from God by a questioning Nicodemus (John 3:2); and as an innocent man by the pagan procurator, Pilate (Luke 23:4, 14; John 18:38; 19:4). And the Philippian jailer recognized that God was with Paul and Silas (Acts 16:37–34). In light of the fact that God can use others to encourage believers, the believer can be assured that even when we are timid God can use our very presence and demeanor to speak to others through our committed lives.

Interestingly, God also can speak through complete strangers to encourage us in our faith.

2. God Speaks through Other Believers

If God can use non-believers to confirm to believers that their life reflects the presence and joy of the Lord, how much more so can God use believers to do this? This actually has happened to me on a number of occasions. For example, everyone would affirm that your own family knows you best. One time my good friend told me how she had been speaking with one of my close family members after I had rededicated my life to Jesus at about 25 years of age. In the conversation, my family member told my friend how he could tell how much I had changed. Of course one would expect family to see these things, but what about total strangers or those who may not know you that intimately? A couple of events reflecting this scenario stand out as particularly God-ordained at moments in my life when I needed to hear from him.

The first situation took place shortly after the horrific events of 9/11. During that period I was in my first master's program at Beeson Divinity School in Birmingham, Alabama. I often flew back and forth between Alabama and Canada for my breaks. As most people who have travelled before and after the events of 9/11 know, airport security was heightened exponentially at that time. During one of my trips, I was pulled out of the line by security as I was boarding the plane. I was at first perturbed and then began to get very upset inside. As I went through the extra security protocols, I could feel my temper raising. I thought to myself, "Don't these people know they need me on that plane?! I would do my best to help out if ever needed in the case of a terrorist attack." As an introvert, I also thought of how awkward it was going to be to walk onto a small plane and have everyone staring at me. It is hard to slip onto a plane as a 6'3" man.

After some time, and after everyone else had boarded, the security team finally let me board. Frustrated, and I am sure not looking, and certainly not feeling too "Christ-like," I walked onto the plane. Of course, my seat was halfway back on the plane and had to be the window seat of a three-seat section. As I pointed to my empty seat the couple sitting beside my seat got up and let me sit down next to the window. I had no sooner sat down when the lady sitting beside me asked the strangest of questions. She said, "Are you a Christian?" Caught slightly off guard, and still silently fuming from my security ordeal, I replied, "Yes." It was what she said next that surprised me the most though. She said, "I could tell as soon as you walked onto the plane that you were a Christian." We spent the next couple of hours talking about the goodness of God.

In all honesty, this happened at a moment when I did not feel very Christ-like; however, much like the experience I had with my gym companion, here a believer, through the presence of the Spirit, saw God's goodness and presence in my life. It was God once again speaking to me through this kind and encouraging word from a complete stranger. A more recent event was even more encouraging.

About four years into my time teaching at Lee University I came to a low point in my career. Many things had been going on at work that caused me to question whether God was still with me and whether he was using me the way he had previously. I had not spoken to anyone about this perhaps with the exception of my wife. One day as I was walking to my office to prepare for class, I walked past one of my former students, whom I had had as a freshman. I greeted her and then went on to my office. A few minutes later this student walked into my office and said that she needed to tell me something. I told her to go ahead and talk to me. She then said that as I had walked by her in the hallway she sensed something in the spiritual realm, as though something was around me and following me. She asked God what it was and God spoke to her and said, "That is my goodness and mercy following him." Needless to say in that moment I lost it emotionally. This student had no idea what I had been going through but God had used her to speak to me and speak to the very concerns that I had been having. God was surely with me and protecting me. Indeed, his presence was all around me to the point that other believers could sense it in the spiritual realm.

Conclusion

In every one of these situations, God used other people not for the purpose of offering a prophetic word over my life, as noted in my previous chapter, but rather as a means of encouraging me. I needed to hear God speaking through those people in those moments in order to confirm that God's Spirit was with me and that his "goodness and mercy" were following me (Ps 23:6). Even though we may not be bold enough to always verbally witness for Christ, or even though we may not feel like a Christian at certain times, God is with us and will use us if we yield ourselves to his will. Indeed, the Shepherd of our lives will speak through us and to us at the most unexpected moments. In some cases, when we least expect it, God uses his people to confirm his calling in our lives.

Chapter 6

God Speaks to Confirm Your Calling

GOD PLACING HIS CALLING on one's life is perhaps one of the most important ways God speaks to us. The calling of God takes on many forms. For those of us in ministry we often define "calling" as working fulltime in some form of service for God. While these callings are important, others have been called to the "corner office" to minister in other ways. By no means am I trying to diminish the call to ministry. On the contrary, James, for example, points out that those who are called to teaching ministry will be judged more severely if we fail to live up to that calling (James 3:1). Yet, when seeking to confirm God's call, no matter who it is, or what occupation to which a person is called, knowing that God is with you as you prepare is important whether that be in ministry, business, nursing, engineering, teaching, etc. I know personally that when I was a carpenter I often said that my *calling* was to spread the Gospel, whereas my *occupation* was carpentry.

Not surprisingly an oft-asked question from students is how to determine the calling of God on one's life. In other words, how is God speaking to you to show you his greater plan and purposes for your life? I can only speak from my experiences in this regard. In some cases, a person has aptitudes that lead naturally to a specific calling to fill a need in the Church. Another way to know God's calling is to recognize what our God-given passions are. We can

God Speaks to Confirm Your Calling

also know God's calling by the doors he opens, or closes, for us. Some people receive a prophetic word to confirm a call. While God can, and does, use all of these means to confirm someone's calling, another method God uses is the encouragement of others. Many times God does this to confirm what he has already stirred in you or laid upon your heart. In light of the various ways that God uses to confirm his calling, I would like to unpack exactly what some of these may look like in a person's life.

1. God-given Aptitudes

By aptitudes I mean, how has God gifted you? For example, if you are excellent at music, and that is what God has gifted you with, then you may be called to work in that field in some way. Some may be gifted speakers and as such may be called to teach, be a salesperson, work in politics, or maybe to stand in the pulpit. I know a couple of people who are great communicators who have been called to ministry and pastoral work. On the other hand, if you struggle with a calling that does not match your gifting, perhaps God will aid you in overcoming that deficiency. Moses certainly felt inadequate in his calling to lead the children of Israel out of Egypt because of his inability to speak (Exod 4:10); yet, God had a means of overcoming that by sending Moses' brother Aaron to be his spokesman (Exod 4:15). In these cases, it is important to keep in mind that as a general rule people should not rely on only one factor, but rather a combination to gain a clear direction from God. This was true in Moses' case: God gave Moses a passion to deliver God's people (Exod 2:11-12); God spoke to him through a theophanic appearance (Exodus 3); God gave him miracles as a sign (Exod 4:1-9); and God brought someone alongside of him to aid him where he was deficient (Exod 4:14-16). For me, God used my ability to organize and teach, along with my resolve to complete whatever I start, to set me on the path of education. Ironically, he overcame my introverted nature (and fear of public speaking), and over a period of time he took away my dislike of reading and writing. God also changed my passions.

2. Our Passions

One's passions can be defined simply as: what drives us to get up in the morning? For a period of time in my life, building was my passion. As an introvert, who did not like being around people and crowds, this suited me well. I could go off to a building site and work for twelve hours by myself. This made me perfectly happy. What is interesting in this regard is that when God began to stir my spirit to change careers, he brought out some of my latent gifts such as teaching and changed my passions. Carpentry no longer was exhilarating for me. On the other hand, I found myself reading and studying God's Word more and more frequently. Biblically we see a fine example of combined passions, aptitudes, and changed careers in the life of David and Paul. First, God took David from following sheep to leading the nation. However, God still used David's skills as a shepherd to lead his people. Also, David was gifted in music and song writing (e.g., the Psalms; 2 Samuel 22). God used these to minister to the nation and to Saul (1 Sam 16:17-23). In this case, God used both David's calling and giftings to help God's people. In Paul's case, Paul went from a persecutor of the Church to a faithful minister of the Gospel to the Gentiles. God used Paul's knowledge of the Scriptures (Acts 22:3; Phil 3:5-6) to formulate almost half of the New Testament and set forth Church doctrine. God also prepared Paul for his task of ministry to the Roman Empire by allowing Paul to be born a Roman citizen. This gave him privileges not afforded to a non-citizen (Acts 22-23). Finally, Paul's training as a tent maker allowed him to provide for himself while doing ministry (Acts 18:3).

3. Opened Doors

Another way to know that God is speaking to you and confirming his call is through opened and closed doors. For a long time I did not know if God would open the doors for me to go to Bible College. When I finally applied and was accepted I was not sure how God would provide. I had run my own carpentry business

God Speaks to Confirm Your Calling

for almost a decade and always made sure all my bills were paid before they were due. With my acceptance into Bible school I struggled with how I was going to pay for this new endeavor with only being able to work over my breaks and during the summer. As someone learning how to listen to God's voice I did the only thing I knew to do based upon the biblical text. Like Hezekiah who took the letter of Sennacherib and laid it before God in the temple seeking God's direction (2 Kgs 19:14), I, too, literally took the acceptance letter for school and laid it before God on the altar of my home church. I prayed for God's direction and felt God impressing upon me that he would provide. I was not sure what that actually meant. I knew I had enough money set aside for a little more than one semester's tuition.

God's opening and closing of doors as well as his provision would be his way of speaking to me in this situation. This became clear when I went through the hoops of filling out the paperwork for student loans to cover my second semester. I sent the paperwork to the leading administrator at the school in order for him to sign them and send them on to the government for processing. About midway through the second semester I received a note from the financial office informing me that my payment for the second semester was late. I could not figure out what the issue was because I had allowed plenty of time for the paperwork for my loans to be processed. Upon further investigation, the chief administrator realized that he had lost my student loan application among the many papers on his desk. His administrative team called me into his office and told me that because it was their mistake they would give me a scholarship covering most of that second semester. I was able to come up with the balance and paid off the second semester.

In the midst of all of this financial confusion, God once again reminded me of what he had impressed upon me earlier in the summer as I prayed at the altar of my church in the middle of a weekday: he would provide. Right then I knew that God had closed the door for me relying on financial aid and that he was going to provide financially. From that time forward, throughout thirteen years of schooling I never had to take out a student loan. I actually finished my entire time in school financially in the black. While this is not necessarily the way God will work for everyone, for me, this opening and closing of doors confirmed that God was with me in my choice to go into fulltime study and eventually a career in ministry.

Another way God opened doors and confirmed my calling was by means of my abilities, which my professors saw in me and in my work ethic. At the beginning of my undergraduate degree I was still unsure in what area of ministry I would ultimately find myself; would it be missions, the classroom, or maybe as an educated Sunday school teacher? Here again is where God can change one's passions and open doors. By my third year of undergraduate work God had opened the doors for me to be a TA and an exam facilitator for the chief administrator of the school. As I began working with the professor and helping my fellow students prepare for tests and exams God gave me not only a desire to teach the Bible but he also gave me a passion to disseminate material in such a way that students could grasp it. When I saw my fellow students' eyes light up with that eureka moment when they grasped the material, God confirmed in me what he had been stirring in my heart for five years. I would perhaps one day become a professor.

4. A Prophetic Word

While I cannot recall ever receiving a direct prophetic word confirming my call to ministry, now, some twenty-five years after God began to stir my spirit about going to Bible school I can say that the prophetic experiences I noted in chapter 4 above were all a part of God's greater plan for my life and my calling. Sometimes it is hard to see the beginning from the end. Now I recognize that the prophetic word about the "closed book" of my life led to the *opening* of another "book" in my life, namely, that of becoming a professor. I encourage my readers always to be open to the prophetic word spoken into one's life. God has given the prophetic gift for the edification not only of the Church, but also of the individual believer (cf. 1 Cor 12:28; 14; Eph 3:5; 4:11).

5. The Opinion of Others

Returning to my discussion in part 2 above, important to my ongoing discussion is the fact that others confirmed the calling of both David and Paul. On the one hand, God used Samuel, Jonathan, and Saul to confirm David's calling to the kingship of Israel (1 Sam 16:13; 23:17; 24:20 respectively). On the other hand, both Jesus (through a vision) and Ananias confirmed Paul's call to ministry in the Church (Acts 9:1–8; 10–20 respectively). When my wife went through the discernment process for going into the ministry a group of godly leaders from her denomination met with her multiple times to help give direction and confirm the voice of God speaking to her to proceed with her schooling and ordination. Many times this outside confirmation can be very helpful. From a personal perspective, this was an important factor in determining my calling. God used a couple of people to confirm what he was doing in my life related to my calling.

When I first was getting to know my good friend Sandie (shortly after she had accepted Christ) she would often come to my home and sit and ask questions about the Bible. At the time I did not realize that I was discipling her. As she continued to grow in Christ she soon felt the desire to go to Bible school. Over a period of several months, she began to stress the fact that I needed to go to Bible school as well and become a teacher. I was pretty settled in my career as a carpenter but it just so happened that God was speaking to my heart at the same time and causing me to want to do more for the Kingdom of God. Over the next two to three years, God consistently used my friend to confirm that God had indeed called me to be more than a builder of houses: God wanted me to be a "builder" of people.

When I finally yielded to God's working on my life I began to consider seriously a life of fulltime ministry. On one visit to the school, which would eventually become the school I attended for my undergraduate degree, God used an evangelist to deliver a message that confirmed what God had laid on my heart. While I cannot recollect all the details of that sermon I do recall that it was like all the people in the room had left and the preacher was speaking directly to me and to me alone. Everything that God had been prompting in my spirit related to my change in careers was confirmed by the ministry of this evangelist during that sermon.

The second person God used to confirm my calling came two years after I started teaching. Even though at this time I was sure of what God had called me to do (see further accounts below), God actually used my mom, my spiritual mentor, to confirm definitively that that calling was not just for a lifetime, it was generational. To a degree, this is similar to David's initial calling by Samuel and then Jonathan's and Saul's confirmation of it much later. Even after David had settled into the kingship of Israel, God sent Nathan the prophet to confirm that his calling to the throne was generational (2 Samuel 7).

In the fall of 2012, my mom was diagnosed with terminal stomach cancer. At that time I was living in Tennessee and my mom lived in New Brunswick, Canada. Because of the distance, I spoke with my mom every day during that time via Skype. Before she passed away, however, my wife, daughter, and I went to visit my mom one last time. After a few days of emotional visitation it was time for me to return to my job in Tennessee. After everyone left my mom's room I returned to give her one last kiss and to say my final goodbyes in person. As I sat on the edge of the bed my mom revealed a "word" she had received from God many years earlier. In a time of prayer when she was a young mother she had been concerned whether or not her devotion to God in taking her children to church would yield eternal spiritual dividends. Some members of the extended family had scolded my mom saying that she was wasting her time dragging her children to church—after all, some of the children, at least at that time, had walked away from God already. That night when my mom was doing her devotions God gave her a word from Jeremiah 35. The account in this chapter deals with the faithfulness of the Rechabites and their dedication to keep the teachings of their father, Rechab. Because of their faithfulness, the prophet Jeremiah told Jonadab, the son of Rechab, that "he would not lack someone to stand before the

Lord always" (35:19). In that moment, my mom knew that God was speaking to her. She felt God telling her that because of her faithfulness to Christ and her faith in God—the faith that had been passed to her from her parents—she would always have someone from her lineage to minister before God. Now I want to be clear, my mom was not the type of person who received a new revelation every other day. Our family knew that when God spoke to her, it was a genuine event. We had witnessed the fulfillment of God's spoken words to my mom on too many occasions.

My mom then looked at me and told me that she had always wanted to go to Bible school and be a teacher but her commitment to raising a family and the prohibitive costs had not allowed her to do so. Then she said that God had fulfilled that promise in me and my calling to teach this generation about the Bible. I cannot tell you how heavily that weighed upon me at that time, and continues to do so (in a positive way). God had used my mom on her deathbed to confirm all that I had been working for over a period of fifteen years.

Conclusion

In light of these examples of how God confirms our calling, I encourage my reader to know of a certainty that God will speak to us to confirm whatever he has laid on our hearts to do for the Kingdom of God. The reality is that we need to surround ourselves with those who are used by God and are godly men and women. We also need to listen closely to how God is speaking and what doors he is opening for us to walk through. When we begin to examine all of these different means by which God speaks, then knowing what God has planned for our lives becomes much easier. And when we still are not sure God is speaking to us then pray that God will speak to us through other means as well. For me, one of these has been God-inspired dreams.

Chapter 7

God Speaks through Dreams and Visions

DREAMS AND VISIONS ARE a common method by which God speaks to people in the Bible especially in the Old Testament period. The book of Ezekiel alone contains four key visions that reveal the plans of God for his people (Ezekiel 1–3; 8–11; 37:1–14; 40–48). A similar method of God's revelation appears in the books of Daniel (Dan 2:19; 7:2; 8:1–27; 9:1–27; 10:7–21) and Amos (Amos 7:1–9; chs. 8–9). As part of the outpouring of God's Spirit in the final days in the book of Joel, the prophet tells his audience that people would see visions and have dreams (Joel 2:28). Not surprisingly one sees a common occurrence of visionary experiences among those of the early church in the book of Acts (Acts 9:10–12; 10:3–20; 11:5; 16:9–10; 18:9–10). On the other hand, dreams, as opposed to visions, tend to be more common in the life of Joseph, the father of Jesus (Matt 1:20; 2:12–15, 19–23; cf. Pilate's wife in 27:19). Many of the dreams in the Bible reveal what is coming in the future or tell the audience or recipient what they should do. Joseph's dreams in Genesis immediately come to mind in this regard (Gen 37:6–10).

Based upon these biblical precedents, it is clear that praying for God to speak to you through dreams and visions is a valid way to hear from God. Similar to the way God uses dreams in the Bible,

God Speaks through Dreams and Visions

I have found that God has used dreams at periods in my life to prepare or warn of things to come. The only drawback of receiving dreams is the problem of interpreting them and distinguishing what is a dream from God and what is a dream instigated from the stresses of life or the result of the proverbial "too much pizza" the night before. I have found that the best way to understand if one's dreams are from God is to allow God to give the interpretation (I will address how this is done below). Dreams can be God's way of speaking directly to us in a very memorable way. Indeed, while the spoken word can stay with you for a long time, dreams and visions have a way of indelibly etching a scene on your memory for life! In my life, this is certainly the case in five different situations. Two deal with the future, two relate to the spiritual struggles in my life, and one deals with preparing me for coming loses.

1. Dreams of the Future

Back in the summer of 1988 God gave me a dream that has stayed with me to this day. It was early in the morning and the dream began with me standing outside on a cloudy day. As I looked up into the sky, the sky began to change color from horizon to horizon. It lit up in a number of hues like red, green, and yellow. I was filled with awe and wonder yet at the same time I sensed a foreboding. In many ways, there are a number of parallels between what I saw and what Ezekiel saw in his first chapter. Interestingly, and unbeknownst to me at the time, Ezekiel would be a portion of the Bible I would later study very closely for my PhD dissertation. As my gaze was drawn to the zenith of the firmament the clouds began to ripple and peel back like a scroll in each direction. Then a cross appeared in this opening in the clouds. Everything was moving quickly in what could best be described as a time-lapse format. At this point the entire sky and atmosphere turned to a warm yellowish hue. What was unique about the hue is that I could actually feel it. It was at this moment that I was made aware in my dream what was actually happening: I was experiencing the rapture/Second Coming of Christ! As I realized this, I began to call out to God in prayer in my dream. I also looked around and realized that there were people running everywhere. I tried to get their attention and tell them that this was the end: Jesus had returned. While I realize that the Bible speaks about Jesus' coming as happening like lightening (Matt 24:27) and things changing in the twinkling of an eye (1 Cor 15:52), at this point in my dream the time-lapse perspective had slowed down to slow motion. In that moment I felt helpless. There was nothing more I could do to prepare for this momentous event. Those who had rejected Christ had sealed their fate. Up to this point, all of this had been overwhelming to my senses and hard to explain. Even now I am searching for words to describe what I saw. In this vein, I can appreciate why Ezekiel constantly used the phrase "it was *like* x or y" to explain what he saw when he witnessed his theophany. In my dream, however, I did not see Jesus but merely the effects of his return. God had saved the proverbial "best for the last" even though my senses were being pushed to their limits and my emotions were beginning to overwhelm me. The yellow hue became stronger and I could feel the tangible presence of the hue settling over my body beginning at my head. As it slowly worked its way down my body I could feel it stop just below my knees and then grasp my legs. I felt myself being lifted off the ground! I was being translated! Unfortunately at that very moment I awakened from my dream and was fully alert to the surroundings in my room.

This dream was so troubling and overwhelming to me that I went and shared it with my pastor. At that time, I felt God impressing upon me the message of the dream: time is short and people should be careful not to put off accepting Jesus. When my pastor heard what I had seen in my dream, he insisted I tell the church, which I did. In the months that followed, every time I told people about my dream I was emotionally broken up. Later that summer, while I was ministering at a youth camp, in one of the evening services, my pastor asked me to tell the campers what I had experienced in my dream. That night many people responded to the pastor's call to prepare their lives to meet God. In the decade that followed that dream I was not sure how I could respond in a meaningful way to what I had seen. As a carpenter I did not have many opportunities to share my dream. While I told others about it whenever the door opened to do so, these opportunities were rare, especially as time went on. Now, looking back almost thirty years later, I realize that God has brought me to a place in my new career where I can tell others on a daily basis about the urgency of the hour and the inevitability and quickness of Jesus' return. While I may not always share what I saw in the dream, I do teach my classes with an urgency of Christ's return.

Now to be sure, some may argue that this dream means nothing and that I am literally "dreaming" things about the coming of Jesus. Before one draws that conclusion, however, I need to follow up on the above account by noting that about four years after that dream I had almost the exact same dream again. After that second dream God gave to me an even clearer interpretation of it. God impressed upon me again that, yes, Jesus was coming soon and that many people would reject Jesus and his message. In these cases, those who chose this path would lose out on the promise of heaven. I want my reader to note that my dream in no way contradicted Scripture but rather corroborated what has already been clearly revealed (cf. Matt 24:30–31; 1 Cor 15:51–53; 1 Thess 4:16–17; Titus 2:13 etc.). All I saw was a few more of the details of what the return of Christ *may* look like. Of course, as already noted above, dreams that come in pairs usually have not only spiritual significance, but point to the fact that what is seen will in fact come to pass. While my life may not have always reflected the urgency of these dreams, they have never left me and I draw upon them regularly when teaching others.

2. Dreams about Our Spiritual Struggle

This second category encompasses a number of my dreams that have a similar theme, namely, the reality that we wrestle not with flesh and blood but against principalities and powers and rulers of the darkness and spiritual wickedness in high places (Eph 6:12).

Hearing the Voice of God

When you desire to make a change in life and combat the Enemy you can be assured that he will not take it lying down.

Most of my dreams related to this topic follow a similar format: sometime in the middle of the night I will dream that I am under attack by an evil force/entity. As this evil force comes against me I call out to God and proclaim the name of Jesus; for at the name of Jesus, every knee shall bow, in heaven, on the earth, and under the earth (Phil 2:10). Most times I will wake up calling out the name of Jesus for help to defeat the oppressive force. Now while I am thankful that I do not have these types of dreams on a regular basis, they are indeed a part of my life. Although I am in no way trying to equate myself with these great men, I am reminded of Daniel and the spiritual battle he experienced when seeking an answer from God (Daniel 10), or perhaps Paul's spiritual struggle with his thorn in his flesh and the messenger from Satan who buffeted him (2 Cor 12:7).

The final dream in this category came to me only a couple of years ago. I was dealing with a situation that included a confrontation with some people in my life. I was not exactly sure how to deal with the impending situation. That night God gave me a dream. In the dream I suffered two attacks while I was riding a bike: first by a small bear and then a larger bear. I got away from the first attack by the smaller bear and continued down the road on which I was traveling; however, the second, larger, bear pulled me off the road and tried to stop me. I eventually got away from that bear too and continued on, although not on the road on which I had originally been traveling. When I woke up I felt God telling me that the dream was an allegory and that I was to continue on my path even though some people may attempt to deter me or push me from that "path." It was not until later that day and the following weeks that the full meaning of the dream became clear.

The dream represented the people with which I had been having a confrontation earlier. They had attempted to sidetrack me in a particular area of my life. While indeed one person, represented by the smaller bear, had tried to divert me, I went forward with what God had laid on my heart to do. And even though the "larger bear" had pulled me off the metaphorical "road" I had been on, they were not able to deter me from my ultimate goal, which God had set before me. For me this dream was God preparing me for a spiritual battle, which I faced at that time, and continue to face, even today. But knowing that God was with me, and that I was doing what he wanted, helped sustain me both then and now when I have been faced with opposition related to this issue.

3. Preparing for Coming Loss

Sometimes God gives dreams and visions to people to prepare them for some significant change in their lives. Peter's vision of the blanket descending from heaven in Acts 10 prepared him for a change in his perspective related to God's inclusion of the Gentiles in the nascent church. At other times God gives dreams to tell us we need to intercede for others (cf. Acts 9:10–16). In the spring of 2010, my wife and I traveled to the Gambia, West Africa, on a short-term missions and teaching trip. I always hate traveling a long distance from home because if anything happens back home it is virtually impossible to return in time. On the first two nights in the Gambia I had the same dream. In the dreams, my uncle, who was like a second father to me, had passed away. I awakened and prayed each day for my uncle feeling God impressing upon me that he was in need of prayer.

Some, I am sure, would chalk these dreams up to the fact that I was worried about being away from home and an emergency like this happening. Now to be sure, my uncle was indeed aged when this happened. However, a day or so after I had these dreams I received an email from my sister telling me that my uncle had suffered a severe health crisis due to undiagnosed pneumonia. It was so severe that he had to be put into the hospital. I told my sister about my dreams and that I had been praying for him. I then realized why God had given me those dreams; my uncle was in need of prayer. At the same time those dreams began to prepare me for the inevitable: my uncle would not live much longer. Almost two years later to the week, my uncle went to be with the Lord. Those dreams not only became a way for me to pray for the impending physical needs of my uncle and to prepare me for the loss that was coming, but more importantly, they let me know that God was using my dreams to speak to me in times of crisis. On more than one occasion, similar promptings in my dreams have led me to pray for people I had dreamed about who were in some form of trouble or need.

Conclusion

There can be no question that dreams can be very tricky to interpret and understand. As can be seen from my experiences noted above, sometimes they are allegorical in nature (the dream about the bears) and sometimes they are straightforward with the characters in the dream actually being the person(s) who needs prayer (my uncle). A general rule of thumb that I have used to interpret or understand if my dream has been from God is if God impresses upon me the interpretation immediately when I wake up. If this happens then I know the dream was of God. Other times it has to do with the frequency of the dream. As I noted before, dreams coming to me in pairs tend to get my attention. I have found these types of dreams are God's way of getting my attention about something very important.

Chapter 8

God Speaks through the Moving and Prompting of the Spirit

As a Pentecostal I have grown up hearing people speak about the Spirit "leading" someone to do or say this or that. While I can appreciate this spiritual method often used by God to speak to people, I also recognize the dangers of the abuse of this mode of God's communication. It can sometimes be used flippantly to manipulate people. As such, I use and speak about this topic with trepidation and caution. Personally, I will only identify something I do as a genuine "prompting of the Spirit" when I have seen it confirmed by God through someone else. If I do not receive this confirmation, many times I chalk it up to my own "prompting" not the Spirit's.

This is similar to the way I view the "moving of the Spirit." It is easy to identify emotionalism with the "move of the Spirit." Indeed, the Spirit can make someone *emotional*, as the Spirit does to me sometimes when I am in an attitude of worship. While many times this is very genuine, sometimes it is simply human emotions reacting to a sad song, an emotional thought, or a touching word from someone. This is not what I am referring to here when I use the phrase "moved by the Spirit." What I mean is when I not only am moved emotionally in a certain way, but the "moving" is followed by some means of confirmation that the Spirit's moving had a greater purpose. I have also seen the "moving of the Spirit" actually be *the* confirmation I was seeking to some prayer. In order not to be too cryptic in this discussion I will give a few examples of what this has looked like in my life.

1. The Prompting of the Spirit

The prompting of the Spirit can simply be defined as the stirring of the Spirit within you to do something that you had not necessarily planned on doing or would not do under ordinary circumstances. This is a common occurrence in the Bible. During the days of King Jehoash people were *prompted* by God to give to the renovations of the temple (2 Kgs 12:4–5; cf. Exod 25:2). In the days following Jesus' birth, Simeon was led by the Spirit to go to the temple and see Joseph, Mary, and the baby Jesus (Luke 2:27). Also, Jesus was "led by the Spirit" into the wilderness to be tempted (Luke 4:1). This concept is further explained in Paul's teaching. When Paul speaks about Christians being "led by the Spirit of God" (Rom 8:14; cf. Gal 5:16) this includes not only performing godly actions, but being sensitive to the Spirit's direction to meet the needs of others and live as true followers of Jesus.

The Spirit's promptings have happened to me on numerous occasions especially when I am teaching Bible classes. In my freshman classes, generally speaking, I have a set course schedule and lesson plan for a given day. There are, however, times when I will add or remove particular sections of a lesson due to time constraints. On one day during a Bible class in 2017 I had decided to skip over a particular part of my lesson where I would normally share a personal story. The story, which I often use to explain the book of Job, takes about 10–20 minutes to tell. As I was lecturing I walked towards my computer to skip the PowerPoint ahead over the story illustrations. As I stood in front of my laptop computer ready to skip to the next part of the lesson I felt the prompting of the Spirit telling me to share the story. As my mind raced about what I felt I heard, I turned to the class and began telling the story. Several minutes later I finished the account and the class ended.

God Speaks through the Moving and Prompting of the Spirit

I dismissed the class and went to the podium to pick up my stuff to leave. When I turned around a couple of students were standing there. One student thanked me for sharing the story. She said it was exactly what she had been praying about and needed to hear. In this case, God immediately confirmed that it was indeed the prompting of the Spirit that had led me to share the story. I thanked the student and told her that I had not planned on telling the account but that on the spur of the moment the Spirit had prompted me to do so. Later that day as I was answering emails, I found several emails from other students who wanted to let me know that they had needed to hear the story as well. These types of confirmations help me to recognize when God is speaking to me literally to change lesson plans in a split second. Of course, one needs to be attuned to the prompting of the Spirit in these cases. Unfortunately, I have not always been good at following these promptings. Indeed, this is an area in which I continue to grow.

A second time when I responded to the prompting of the Spirit more recently was when I was sending a birthday wish to a student. I regularly send personalized email birthday wishes to students in my classes. Most the time it is a one-line note wishing my student a blessed day. On one particular day as I was sending a note I felt the Spirit telling me to say more than normal. As a matter of fact, I felt the Spirit giving me the words to write as I encouraged the student in God. While it was not a long email, it did get the point across that God loved this student and that they were special. I almost hesitated to send the email because it was so out of character with what I normally sent for a birthday wish. I yielded to the Spirit and hit the send button. Within just a few minutes the student responded and thanked me for the kind words. They said it was exactly what they needed to hear at that moment. I quickly responded and told the student how the Spirit had led me to send the note. Again, this may not seem like much, but to that student, God had used me to speak to her in a very unique way. What is more, God once more helped me to recognize how he moves and speaks to me in a personal way.

Hearing the Voice of God

Sometimes God's prompting can be to do things that make absolutely no sense to you in the moment. As I noted in chapter 6 above, God had impressed upon me that he would provide for my schooling; now that is not to say that when I went to the mailbox that I found money sent to me by a total stranger. On the contrary, in actuality, only on one occasion throughout thirteen years of school did someone give me a card with a substantial monetary gift in it. Instead, God provided work for me and gave me the ability to work long hours as a carpenter throughout my thirteen years of schooling. Interestingly, we also find scriptural evidence that Paul worked side jobs to provide for himself while he ministered to others (cf. Acts 18:1–4; 1 Thess 2:9). This was how God provided for my schooling. While some may see this as no great miracle, for me it was. My schooling took me out of the country and thus out of the spotlight to potential customers back home. Yet people were willing to wait for me to return back home during breaks and in the summer to have their work done. Most of the time during those thirteen years I was booked two years in advance!

This background is important for what God asked of me towards the end of my undergraduate degree. I was sitting in a church service at the college I was attending when a call went out for students and faculty to help with a need in the school (cf. Acts 4:32–37; 24:17; 1 Cor 16:1–4; Phil 4:16–18). It was early in the fall semester and I knew I had one substantial check coming from the last job I had completed during my summer carpentry work. I felt God speaking to me to give this money to the school. I was not one just to give away money I knew I would need to pay my school bills. And I am not suggesting that people should do what God asked me to do. Wisdom and discernment are certainly needed in these situations. Because I had become more attuned to hearing the voice of God, I felt strongly that this was the prompting of God for me to do this thing. When the final check arrived in the mail I signed it over to the school to help meet the need. Not surprisingly, God met my needs for the rest of the semester and school year. Again, I finished that year financially in the black. Please understand; I am not trying to preach a get-rich Gospel punctuated by sowing "seed" into some ministry. While God may lead someone to do this, this type of manipulation is by far too prevalent today in many ministries. What I am trying to present is a way of learning how to hear and respond to the prompting and leading of the Spirit.

Although I could give numerous examples, one final account will suffice to make my point. Back in the late 90s when I was finishing my undergraduate degree in Bible I was in the prayer room one night by myself praying. During my prayer time another person walked into the room. I felt the Spirit prompting me to go and give what I felt was a word from God for that person. Now while those used in this gift may not see this as anything particularly earth-shattering, for me this was completely new. I had never done this before. I nervously walked over and interrupted the person praying and spoke to them what I felt God impressing upon me to say. The person immediately thanked me: it was what they had needed to hear!

2. The Moving of the Spirit

Another way that God can speak to someone is through the moving of the Spirit. The reason I see this as distinct from the prompting of the Spirit is that the latter tends to be the Spirit urging you to do or say something, as pointed out above; whereas the moving of the Spirit, at least in the way I am using it here, is when God breaks into your normal, everyday, world and interrupts it for a greater purpose or to give direction to you or someone else. Many would place the charismata in this category (glossolalia, a message of discernment, prophecy, the gift of helps etc. cf. 1 Cor 12:4–10). When God comes upon me in this way, it tends to be in the realm of my emotions. While the Spirit moves on people in many different ways, for me, the Spirit tends to break me emotionally causing me to weep. As an introvert, it seems as though the Spirit likes to move me in this way at what I feel are the most inopportune moments.

Last year I was in the very first freshmen Old Testament Survey class of the semester when God decided to move on me in a special way. Like many professors, the first day of class is the day in the semester when professors "lay down the law" for the semester and pass out the syllabus. I walked into the class and introduced myself and started to open the class in a word of prayer. As I began to pray the Spirit broke me and I began to weep. Immediately I was taken aback. This had never happened to me before. While I may get emotional telling a story, I had never gotten emotional on the opening day of class before, especially on the day I was discussing the syllabus! I attempted to pull myself together and finish my prayer. I quickly apologized to the class and explained that what had just happened was not the normal way I teach a class. In that moment I could not figure out what God was doing. Slightly embarrassed, I went on to complete the class and pick up my stuff to leave. While I was doing this, one of the students walked up to me and in a sincere and serious tone she said, "Thank you!" I said, "For what?" She proceeded to explain to me that she had come to the class praying to God that he would show her what the moving of the Spirit looked like. Immediately everything made sense. God had broken into my class and had used me to answer someone else's prayer. The interesting thing about that particular class is that throughout the semester I felt a freedom in the Spirit to teach and minister to the students in a very special way. And it had all begun with the Spirit breaking into my class during an opening prayer!

One final account will help show how God used this spiritual phenomenon when I was making an important decision for my family. When I first moved to Cleveland, TN, my wife and I set about the task of finding a church home. My wife comes from an Anglican/Episcopal tradition and, as I have noted before, I am Pentecostal. Also of importance is the fact that Cleveland is in the heartland of the Bible belt and particularly the Church of God. With a church on almost every corner, my wife and I had many churches to choose from. We were both in prayer as we began visiting churches to find a permanent church home. We went to almost a dozen different churches looking for the right fit. At one point in this process my wife and I began to get somewhat frustrated. I asked God to help us and show me where he wanted us.

God Speaks through the Moving and Prompting of the Spirit

Within a week or so my wife and I went to visit a church associated with the Church of God. As I stood in the service and listened to the songs being sung, God began to move upon me by his Spirit. I stood there and wept before God. While I am not trying to diminish any of the other churches we had visited, for me I knew this was perhaps God showing me where to settle my family. However, wanting to be sure, we continued looking but found ourselves back at the same church a few weeks later. The exact same thing happened again during the time of worship and singing. With this second moving of the Spirit upon my heart, I felt sure that God was confirming that this was where we were to be. We have been at this church now for seven years and have found that it has met many of our needs at this time.

Conclusion

The prompting and moving of the Spirit is an important way that God uses to speak to his people. However, as I have noted throughout this chapter, caution must be exercised when identifying what is the true prompting of the Spirit as opposed to what is coming from one's own heart (see chapter 2 above). Learning to hear God's voice in the midst of the busyness of our lives takes work. I have found that asking for God to use me in this fashion helps prepare me to be alert to those gentle, but all-important, promptings. When you begin to experience the moving and prompting of the Spirit, you will wonder how you lived life without it. Of course, like anything else, if we neglect something long enough we can get out of practice and in the case of hearing the Spirit's voice, we can get spiritually "rusty." Constant communion with God is the best remedy for this.

Chapter 9

God Speaks through Events

THE BIBLE IS REPLETE with narrative accounts showing that God uses circumstances and events in people's lives to show that he is with them or leading them even though they may not sense God speaking directly to them in the moment. The lives of people like David, Ruth, and Esther are prime examples of this way of God's speaking and leading people. David was not told by God to kill a giant (1 Samuel 17) but the reader knows it is God using him for this victory. Or consider how God protects David as he spends time on the run from Saul; clearly God is with him even though David lives out his life and makes decisions to the best of his abilities. Next, not once does the reader see the name of God in the book of Esther but it is clear that his fingerprints are all over the events of Esther's life. Also, the life of Ruth certainly shows that God works in the midst of unexpected circumstances to bring blessings and no doubt answers to prayers. The verse found in Proverbs 16:9 comes to mind in these cases: "A person makes their plans in their heart but the Lord directs his paths."

Of course, readers can see that God is at work in the lives of biblical characters because we can read the accounts of these individual's lives in their entirety in one sitting, if we so desire. In other words, we can see the beginning from the end. In the believer's everyday life this becomes very problematic because we are living in the *midst* of what God is doing in our lives. I have found that God often uses circumstances and events in my life that only later become clear in light of God's greater purposes. Indeed, in some cases it is only later that I realize that these events were God's way of speaking to me. In light of these types of circumstances, I have concluded that God's working through events can be a very important and meaningful way of God speaking to his people. Several clear examples of this have happened in my life over the past number of years.

Trusting God to Lead

My educational years spanning from my undergraduate work to my PhD are filled with God's working through events in my life in order to speak to me and let me know that he is in control of my steps. The event, which is of particular importance to my theme of this chapter, took place during my second master's program. As I was finishing my Master of Old Testament degree at Gordon-Conwell Theological Seminary, I and many of my fellow students began making application to schools for PhD work. One of my former professors had suggested I apply to the University of Toronto because I was a Canadian. So, feeling that this was a good idea, I applied to that university. As the winter wore on and gave way to the spring, my friends started receiving responses to their applications. One day when I was speaking with one of my friends they asked me how many schools I had applied to. This question caught me slightly off guard. You see, up until that time I had only ever applied to one school at a time. I would feel that God was leading me to apply to a particular school and so I would apply there. I had always gotten accepted at the particular school to which I had applied. Now, I am not trying to belittle those who apply to multiple schools it is just that this was the way God had worked in my life. I did not know any different way of doing it. I truly had trusted in the direction of God in this regard.

My friend went on to tell me that she had applied to about a half dozen schools just in case she did not get accepted at her first choice of schools. You can imagine what I felt like knowing that I had applied to only *one* school! Immediately doubt began to enter my mind. I had never had this experience since first being accepted into my undergraduate program. What if I did not get accepted into a PhD program? I began to try to imagine alternative possibilities for my immediate future. Perhaps I could do another master's program I thought. Maybe I would have to return home and work for a year. I went to the mailroom to see if I had received any word from the school about my application. There was nothing in my mailbox. My mind began to race. I chided myself thinking, "How could I have been so stupid not to apply to more places?" Now the deadlines for applying to schools were long since passed.

As I walked back to my apartment I felt like I should call the University of Toronto (I would later realize that this was the prompting of God—see last chapter). The problem was who would I call? Anyone who is familiar with the University of Toronto system knows that the university is massive with almost 90,000 students spread over numerous schools, colleges, and departments. I had applied to Wycliffe College and Knox College within the Toronto School of Theology. But who should I call? I went online and found the phone number to the Toronto School of Theology (remember I was shooting blind here, or so I thought). I dialed the number and a secretary answered the phone. I asked how I could find out about the status of an application. She responded that I would need to talk to the Toronto School of Theology director. She then proceeded to ask if I wanted my call to be transferred to his office; I responded in the affirmative. Within seconds I was talking to the director. I politely asked if there was any way of finding out about the status of my application. He asked for my name and then he hesitated. He said, "You say your name is Brian Peterson?" I said, "Yes." He continued, "Peterson . . . Peterson . . . just a second." I could hear him rustling some papers. He then came back on the phone and said, "Interesting. Your application is in the stack of applications that I am taking to my meeting in a few minutes to discuss." He then said, "I can call you in a couple of hours and let you know of our decision." Needless to say that was the longest two hours of my life as I sat by the phone waiting for his response.

As promised, two hours later the director called, and you guessed it, he said I was accepted based upon the recommendation of Dr. Frank Thielman from Beeson Divinity School. I thanked him and said goodbye. Of course the director did not realize what had just happened, but I did. What are the odds of what had just transpired? This is once again why I do not believe in coincidences in such matters. Needless to say, I finished my MAOT with much less stress of where I would be going the next year.

My naiveté in how PhD programs worked was also on display when I had to choose one of the two schools at which to matriculate: Wycliffe College or Knox College. I had heard about John Wycliffe when taking Church history so I chose Wycliffe College. I know this does not sound very spiritual but God was still with me in my ignorance. I was assigned to a PhD director, Dr. Glen Taylor, who not only was one of the very few faculty members at the TST with whom I resonated theologically, but who also became a close friend. Moreover, his wife, Dr. Marion Taylor, another OT professor, became a mentor and friend as well. Looking back on it now, and knowing all of the theological positions of the numerous colleges in the TST, Wycliffe College and the Taylors were a perfect fit for my educational plans. God had been merciful to me in the midst of my naiveté to place me exactly where he wanted me.

2. God's Leading to Help Others

My final two examples deal with how God works through events in my life. The first one happened in the summer of 2017 while I had a team of Lee University students in Israel doing archaeology at the ancient site of Shiloh. My team arrived from the USA at our hotel in Jerusalem on a Friday afternoon. Because the actual dig did not begin until Monday, we arranged to go on a tour with our dig director early on Saturday morning. When we got up in the morning to leave we realized that there were not enough seats in the van for everyone. It ended up that two of my students and I had to remain behind. The three of us decided to do a walking tour of the old city of Jerusalem.

Before relating the interesting events that transpired over the next few hours I need to give a few details about my experience as a "tour guide" in Jerusalem, and the two students who went with me. First, on the past trips to Israel, I had only toured the old city with the help of someone else. I had never led a group. Although I knew the layout of the larger part of the old city, I did not know where to find a lot of the attractions (e.g., the Church of the Holy Sepulcher; the Via Delarosa; the Wailing Wall etc.). Therefore, most of my "tour guiding" was walking through the old city and stumbling upon important sites or asking direction in order to find them. I knew that if I could find a gate in the old city I could walk around the perimeter until I found the Damascus Gate, which was a landmark I knew well enough to find my way back to the hotel. The second point of interest relates to the details about the majors of the two female students who were with me. One student was a French major and the other student was taking music theory—the importance of these details will become clear shortly.

We walked to the old city and began our approximately three-hour tour. As lunch time approached, we decided to return to the hotel. We headed to the nearest gate in the old city walls. As we walked towards the Dung Gate I stopped for a few moments and pointed out to my two students some of the ruins of the Temple Mount. This literally was only for a couple of minutes at the most. As we turned to leave, out of the corner of my eye I saw a woman trip and fall on the cobblestone road causing her water bottle to fly out of her hand and roll down the street. My two female students ran to her aid immediately and I joined them a few seconds later. As they helped her to her feet the three began to converse. She was from France, and you guessed it, my French major immediately began to converse with her and put her at ease. The lady could speak some English so when she realized that we were "friends" and could be trusted she began to open up to us and tell us a bit about herself. Within just a few minutes we realized that she was a Christian. We told her that we were Christians as well and that I

God Speaks through Events

worked at a Christian university and the ladies were my students. She told us that she was a music theorist! Immediately she had a connection to both of my students: one spoke French like her and one studied music theory like her, and of course, all four of us were Christians.

While all of this could be attributed to mere coincidence, what happened next shattered that conclusion. All of these "coincidences" set her at ease to the point that she opened up and told us that she was scared to walk back to her hotel because she had to take a street where she had been mugged a couple of years earlier. I stepped forward and asked her if she would like to walk with us because we were going in the same direction. I am in no way trying to brag, but in full disclosure to those reading, I am 6'3" and 220 pounds and a former bodybuilder. She quickly accepted my offer. She proceeded to tell us that just before she met us she had been praying to God that he would protect her. We walked through the Dung Gate and skirted the city walls. She told us that she was planning on going to Shiloh the next day. Of course, this was another point of contact. We told her we were doing archaeological work at the site. We boldly walked by a number of local men and our French friend talked with us freely. When we reached her street we said our goodbyes and parted company never to see her again.

I walked on for a few minutes with my students and then stopped and asked them, "Do you know what just happened?" I began to show them how God had used us to answer a complete stranger's prayer. From earlier that morning, God had instigated and engineered every part of what had happened. All of these factors could not be a coincidence. First, the two students who did not have a seat on the bus were female—something that set our female French friend at ease. Second, their majors were French and music theory, two more connections. Third, I was leading them; I was large and, so they tell me, intimidating, something that our French friend appreciated given the circumstances. Fourth, we chose to leave the old city by exiting the exact gate through which this lady was walking. Fifth, we stopped just long enough to view ancient ruins at the place where we would meet. Sixth, our French friend tripped at the right time to make the connection. Seventh, she had been praying for protection and God used us to provide it for her.

The final example I would like to relate took place early in 2018. One day when I was driving into work I decided not to park in my usual parking spot or parking lot due to the heavy rain that was falling that day. Instead, I parked just off the campus grounds, yet as close to my office as possible. Later that day I had to go back home for an hour or so to keep the kids while my wife came in and taught her class at the university. As I was walking to my vehicle with my umbrella blocking the rain I just happened to walk in front of the car of one of my students (I did not know this at the time though). Due to the heavy rain I had my head down with my umbrella shielding my face. At that moment I just happened to look up long enough to notice my student sitting in her car. I could see that she was crying about something. I stopped and asked what the problem was. She said she had been praying about a need and I could see that she was somewhat distraught about it. I immediately sensed that God wanted me to be the answer to this student's prayer. I told her to leave her prayer/request with me. Later, I was able to tell her that my wife and I would help answer her prayer. Once again God had orchestrated my paths without me even knowing it. All of the events of that day from the rain, to my choice of parking lot, to my having to go home early to relieve my wife, to my looking up from my umbrella at the right time all coalesced for the purpose of helping to answer the prayer of one of my students.

Conclusion

These types of events demonstrate the text that says the steps (sometimes literally) of a righteous person are ordered by the Lord (Ps 37:23). God uses events and circumstances in our lives to show that he is in control and that he uses his children for his greater purposes. What these types of events show us is that God can, and does, speak to us through events if we are paying attention to how he works in the lives of believers. Admittedly, hindsight is always

God Speaks through Events

20/20 and seeing God at work sometimes requires one to reflect back on the circumstances and past events. In the case of my tour through Jerusalem, it only took a few minutes of reflection on the events of the previous few hours to quickly realize that God was at work. Sometimes it takes days, months, or even years to connect all the God-ordained dots and see his marvelous direction. In light of these realities, I challenge my reader to examine your life and to ask the question that has become a part of my Christian walk: "What are the odds?" What are the odds that certain circumstances/events happen in your life? I am a firm believer that with God, there are no coincidences in the life of the Christian!

Chapter 10

God Speaks through Signs

GENERALLY SPEAKING, GOD'S USE of signs to speak to his people comes in two different formats. First, there are signs that God initiates himself in order to speak to people and to confirm a particular aspect of his plan for humanity. One of the more well-known signs in this category is quoted regularly at Christmas time: "Therefore the Lord Himself will give you a sign: Behold, a virgin will be with child and bear a son, and she will call His name Immanuel" (Isa 7:14; NASB). Signs addressed to the people of Israel also appear in the book of Ezekiel and in the Gospel of John. In these latter two cases, Yahweh uses the prophet Ezekiel to give signs of God's coming judgment (Ezek 4:3; 12:6, 11; 14:8; 24:24, 27) and Jesus uses signs to convince the people of Israel that he is the Son of God (John 1:7; 20:31). God also sent the plagues through the word of Moses as signs to the Egyptians—and by extension to Israel—to show that he was the only true God (Exodus 7–12). The second category is a sign asked for by an individual to prove that God is leading them to make a particular decision or undertake a specific action. Gideon is a prime example of seeking for a sign from God in order to know that God was leading him. Before going into battle against the Midianites, Gideon asked for two signs using a fleece. In both cases, God confirmed his plans by giving Gideon the requested signs (Judg 6:38–40). Closely connected to the use of signs is the casting of lots (1 Sam 14:41–42; Acts 1:26); whereby God uses a very natural process to give direction. The priestly use of the Urim and Thummim may also fall into this category (Exod 28:30; Lev 8:8; Num 27:21; Deut 33:8; 1 Sam 28:6; Ezra 2:63 etc.).

It is the second category of signs that I would like to examine in this chapter. When I speak of seeking for a sign from God I do so with a level of caution. I am not speaking about frivolously asking God for a sign like allowing the wind to blow the curtains a certain way to confirm my decision about where to take my wife on a date or for the fifth car that passes my house to be blue to confirm what outfit I should wear for a job interview. On the contrary, the signs that I have asked God for in the past are generally related to major decisions I am making in life. Much like Gideon wanted to confirm the word of the angel of the Lord by two signs, when, and if, I ask for a sign it is to confirm something I feel God has already shown me or laid upon my heart. I will give two examples to demonstrate how this has played itself out in my life.

A Sign to Change My Career

As I have noted elsewhere in this book, when I felt God stirring my heart to change my career and go to school full time I wanted to be sure that this was God speaking. Although others had encouraged me in this endeavor, and even though God had used the prophetic voice to show me that things were going to be changing in my life, I wanted to know for sure that God was specifically leading me to go to Bible school. Knowing the account of Gideon, I asked God for a specific sign to confirm his word. I sent my application to Zion Bible College and asked God that if the school accepted me without conditions (among other concerns and issues, I had been out of high school for close to ten years at that time) then I would know that he was leading me in this direction. Within just a few weeks of making application to Zion, I received a full acceptance without conditions. I knew that this was a sign from God that I was to move forward and make plans to attend school in the fall. And as they often say, the rest is history.

A Sign to Get Married

The next three signs deal with my decision to get married. Throughout my time in school I dated a number of very wonderful ladies; most of the time my dating life amounted to no more than one or two dates, although in one case I dated for several months. In an attempt to guard my heart and not to awaken love before its time (Song of Solomon 2:7; 3:5; 8:4), I continually asked God to close doors to relationships that were not part of his perfect plan/will. I knew that as a future professor in ministry, it would take a certain type of lady to share in my calling. In the fall of 2006, after God had closed a number of relationship "doors" I met a young woman with whom I "clicked" in a number of areas. She was training for ministry and was a committed Christian who had a similar charismatic experience as I had had. The encounter was not what I had expected, however, because I was Pentecostal and she was part of the Episcopal tradition. I entered the relationship cautiously, but after a period of a few months I sensed that this was a relationship that was different than the others I had experienced up to this point. I asked God for a sign that this was a girl I should pursue beyond a casual dating relationship. Because there was a significant age gap between us, I prayed that if this was what God wanted that when I actually told the girl my age (I hid my age well as an athlete) that it would not be a concern for her. In full disclosure, I had lost more than one potential girlfriend once they found out how old I was. I can remember the night I told her. My heart was pounding. After dropping the proverbial bombshell she looked at me and simply said, "There is a large age difference between my mom and my step-father too." Now to be honest, she did not just pass over this revelation flippantly, but for her it was not a "deal breaker."

Although I had received what I felt was a positive response to the first sign I still wanted further confirmation that this was the girl I should marry. Dating was one thing, but a lifetime commitment was something quite different. I can remember that over the next several months I struggled with God's will regarding my

God Speaks through Signs

relationship with this woman and what our life would look like if we got married. What church would we attend? In what tradition would we raise our children? What would our families say to the union? How would I be received if I taught in a denominational school and my wife ministered in an Episcopal church? These and many other questions rattled around in my head as I finished the spring semester of 2007 and went home to work that summer. My good friends had encouraged me to pop the question when I told them about this amazing girl I had met; but I still was unsure. What if my *feelings* were off? What if they were from me and not pleasing to God? I began to ask God for another sign that he was leading me in this decision.

That second sign came one day as I was driving on the interstate listening to a Christian radio station. Out of the blue the radio host made a statement that confirmed what I had been praying about. He pointed out that many guys have lists of what they want in a girl (and yes, I had a list). He went on to explain that love is so much more than a simple *feeling*—these can, and do, change with time—he said, "Love is a choice." As soon as I heard those words I knew what God was saying to me. I went home that day and ordered an engagement ring!

I would like to say that the hard part was behind me, but being slightly old fashioned, I knew I still had to ask permission from my girlfriend's parents before I could actually get engaged (my girlfriend was twenty-five years old at this time but I still wanted to "do things right"). Once again I asked God for his mercy. I prayed for a third sign. The sign was that when I asked her parents for their blessing on the engagement that they would say yes. Now some may be thinking that this was a mere formality. The truth is a variety of things were working against me: the age gap, the fact that I was Pentecostal and not Episcopal, my wife was called into ministry in the Episcopal Church, and I was from another country. How would this all work out?

I can remember the weekend that I visited my wife's family and the day that I was going to ask for their permission. I was so worked up that I made myself nauseous. When my girlfriend left the house for a short errand, I asked her parents if I could talk with them. With great anxiety and my heart pounding, I asked them if I could have their daughter's hand in marriage. Her step-father said he was okay with it but that the decision was really up to her mom. Her mother looked at me and smiled and said, "Yes." Although we had our fair share of ups and downs over the next few months, Christine and I were married on August 23, 2008. Today we have four beautiful children, and all of those other questions I had, well, God has worked many of them out already in his timing.

Conclusion

God's gracious response to my request for signs confirming that he is leading me has become a viable way that I hear God speaking to me when I am making life-altering decisions. I have not requested signs for every major decision, but when I have God has been faithful. Before ending this chapter it is important to point out that I have asked for signs in other situations and God has responded in the negative. Therefore I want to be clear that signs are not always a simple confirmation. Sometimes the signs turn into closed doors (see above discussion). Whatever response God gives me through my request for signs I have found that this is a very meaningful way that I hear the voice of God in my life.

Chapter 11

God Speaks through a Still Small Voice

UP TO THIS POINT I have covered a number of ways God can speak to people. In every case they have been indirect. Even if God uses the prophetic office to speak to the believer God is nonetheless speaking through a secondary source. Throughout the Bible, God addresses people directly (e.g., Abraham, Moses, Samuel, Elijah, Peter, Paul, the prophets, etc.) and/or through angels (e.g., Joshua, Manoah's wife/Samson's mother, Daniel, Ezekiel, etc.). Apart from God's direct interaction with Moses (cf. Num 12:4–8), perhaps one of the more intimate communications between God and a person is that experienced by Elijah on Mt. Horeb (1 Kgs 19:9–18) after his Mt. Carmel victory against the prophets of Baal (1 Kgs 18:20–40). In a theophany on Mt. Horeb, God came to Elijah not in the wind, an earthquake, or a fire, but in a still small voice (1 Kgs 19:13). The intimate way in which God communicates with his people one-on-one through an audible voice, while perhaps not the norm for every day, or for everybody, is still scriptural and to be expected. I have found that when God has spoken to me in this fashion it is both life-changing and memorable. Furthermore, in my life God normally reserves this type of communication for very special purposes and direction. In what follows, I will look at two very special times when God spoke to me in a very intimate and direct manner: one deals with my plans for the future which relates to my choice of career, and the second deals with my future as it relates to my progeny.

Hearing God's Voice for My Future Career

In my life thus far, I can honestly say that I can recall only one time when God spoke to me in what I would classify as an audible voice. Not surprisingly, this encounter had to do with making a decision that would affect my life for the foreseeable future from a career perspective. This career choice would end up leading me into teaching ministry as a professor.

I was in my fourth year of my undergrad program and trying to decide at which school to do my master's level work, if in fact this was what God wanted for me. One of my friends asked me to go with him and his wife to check out Beeson Divinity School at Samford University in Birmingham, Alabama. The plan was to go visit the school immediately after we got out of classes just before Christmas. When the day arrived that we were to visit the school, it just so happened that the weather had turned stormy. We had traveled most of the way to the school when Birmingham experienced a snow storm. We contacted the school and they told us that the school most likely would not be open due to the inclement weather. We asked if there was any way someone could come in to the school long enough to show us around because we had already traveled so far. They agreed to make arrangements and we got our chance to see the school the next day. I was struggling with moving so far from home. I lived in New Brunswick, Canada at the time and this would mean that in any emergency, I would have a greater distance to travel home. While we were at the school the person in charge tentatively accepted us as students for the following year based upon our GPAs. He told us we also may qualify for full tuition scholarships.

The next day I said goodbye to my friends and went on to visit another friend in Jacksonville, Florida for the Christmas holidays. I told them I would see them back in Rhode Island in a couple of weeks. After my visit in Florida I started my flight back to my

God Speaks through a Still Small Voice

school in RI. My flight had a layover in Philadelphia. Because I had not flown that much up to that point in my life, I had never been in a multi-terminal airport before. I landed in one terminal and then had to take a shuttle to the next terminal. I was somewhat discombobulated due to the switch in terminals. When I finally located my gate I sat down and began to ponder about my future and the fact that the school had accepted me and may even give me a full scholarship. Did God want me to go to Beeson? Did he want me to go on for further schooling at all? How could I pay for my schooling if I did not get a scholarship? I did not want to be out of God's will.

Because I was traveling alone during the Christmas holidays I was somewhat lonely (I was single at this juncture in my life). I also was hungry and wanted to grab a bite to eat, but I did not like eating alone, especially at this time of the year when family and friends are so important. I looked around and saw hundreds of people milling around the terminal but not one person I knew (not that I had expected to see anyone I was familiar with). I no sooner got that thought out of my mind when I turned my focus to the gate where I would be boarding my plane. Just then my good friend with whom I had visited Beeson Divinity School a couple of weeks earlier walked out of the gate with his wife. Now I could easily have been looking down and missed them totally, but God had arranged it so I would see them at that moment. In fact, they came out of the gate through which I was to board and walked past my seat just one row away. I looked at them slightly shocked and spoke their names. They turned and, just as surprised, responded to me. I asked, "What are you doing here?" And my friend answered and said they did not know why they were there. He continued and told me that the airline had rerouted their plane to this airport. They were supposed to have a direct flight back to RI but had ended up in Philadelphia. Just then I remembered what I had thought just moments before about not wanting to eat alone and I smiled and asked them if they were hungry. They said yes. I noticed that my flight had been delayed twenty minutes, just enough time to grab something to eat. After we had eaten, we said our goodbyes again and I went and boarded my plane.

Once the plane taxied out to the runway and we prepared to take off, I began pondering what had just happened. I thought of what the odds were of the events of the past 45 minutes actually happening in a world without God in the picture. It was at that moment that I heard the audible (although inside my head) voice of God which has stayed with me to this day. God said, "I know exactly where you are, I know exactly where you are going. If I can bring your best friends to your airport, to your terminal, and to your gate so you do not have to eat alone, you can trust me with your future." I knew that this was God's way of confirming that I should go to Beeson and allow God to lead my path. A couple of weeks later confirmation of what I had heard while waiting in my plane on the tarmac came when I received word that I had been given a full tuition scholarship to Beeson. God had clearly spoken to me; he had opened the door; and now he had provided the financing for my next two years of schooling!

That word from God has never left me. From that point forward I never questioned God's plan for my life when it came to my schooling. Although I may still have needed to learn some lessons about trusting him to open doors (see above) I knew he would lead me and that I could trust him to bring me to where he wanted me to be. Those words would carry me spiritually through a number of trials throughout my next nine years of schooling and three degrees.

Hearing God's Voice for My Future Progeny

The second event is not focused so much on an audible voice of God but rather on a very strong impression that he placed on my heart from a very young age. Let me explain. I come from a family of eight children: five boys and three girls. Two of the three girls married and had children, which were all boys. Of course my nephews had the last name of their fathers. On the other hand, three of the five boys in my family married. Of the children born to them, none were boys. Therefore my parents did not have any male grandchildren to carry on the family name.

Long before I was married I felt God impressing upon my heart that I would be the one to carry on the family name through male offspring. As the second *youngest* I did not think I would ever have the first male grandchild. Much like Mary pondering in her heart the words concerning Jesus (Luke 2:19, 51), I never told anyone about what I had felt God was impressing upon my heart. When I did get married, my wife and I discussed having children. My wife was an only child. Her father died of terminal brain cancer when she was three years old and therefore also had no male heir to carry on the family name. Before we got married we decided that my wife would keep her last name to honor her father. I also told my wife that if we had two male children one could carry my last name and the second one her father's last name.

Two years into our marriage my wife got pregnant. We decided not to find out the gender of the child until the baby was born. Christine asked me what I thought the child's gender would be. I told her I knew, but that I would not tell her. I was relying on what God had placed upon my heart many years before even though at that point I had not told my wife about what God had showed me. When it came time for her to have our child we had two names ready; one if the child was a girl and one if the baby was a boy. When my *daughter* Madeline was born I was somewhat taken aback. Not only was I not sure what was going on based upon what I had felt God had spoken to me years earlier, but I was also not sure how to be a father to a little girl! Now do not get me wrong I love my daughter dearly, but in that moment I was confused. Of course, I thought I had heard God's voice incorrectly. It would not be until about a year and a half later that everything became clear as to why my first child was a girl.

We named our daughter after my mom's middle name. My mom came to visit us shortly after Madeline was born. It had been years since she had held a grandchild (most of my older siblings had long since finished having children). We also went home for Christmas that year so my family could meet the newest addition to the Peterson clan. My mom was elated. Sadly, when my daughter Maddie was a little over one year old my mom was diagnosed with terminal cancer. Over the next three months we video-chatted by Skype regularly. My mom would always ask to see "her babes," Maddie. Talking with Maddie gave her something to look forward to each day and something to live for as long as possible. Before my mom passed away, my wife and I took our daughter Maddie and flew home to see my ailing mother one last time. I wanted my mother to bless my daughter. I videotaped my mom praying over my daughter. It was an experience much like when Jacob blessed the two sons of Joseph before he died (Gen 48:11–20). My mom passed away about two months later.

In the midst of the pain of losing my mom I began to understand better what God had actually placed on my heart years earlier. He had never said my *first* child would be a boy but only that I would have a male heir. After my mom passed away I realized why Maddie had been born first. My mom got the chance to see her namesake before she died! There was also something else that came out of having a daughter. I realized that there is a bond between a father and daughter that is unique. I always say that Maddie taught me how to love in a very special way.

Within a few months of my mom's passing, my wife got pregnant again. Once again she asked me if I knew what the gender was. This time I hesitated. I continued to ponder in my heart all which God had spoken to me years earlier. When our second child was born it was a boy! Immediately upon seeing that our newborn child was a boy I had to leave the room to go to the washroom to compose myself. I was weeping almost uncontrollably. God had fulfilled his word! At 47 years of age, God had brought to pass what he had laid on my heart almost three decades earlier. My wife and the doctor did not know where I had gone. The doctor began asking who was going to cut the umbilical cord. I shouted out from the bathroom that I would be there in a minute. Later I told my wife why I had been so emotional. God is good!

A little over two years later my wife gave birth to our third child, Kevin. We named him after my wife's father's first and last names. God had given me a double blessing, which started with a special word to me many years before. God had done exceedingly abundantly more than I could have ever imagined. He blessed my family with a beautiful daughter who is named after my mom. My mom was able to see and pass on a special blessing to her namesake before she passed away. He gave me the first male heir of the Peterson line, and he blessed my wife with a son to carry on her father's name. Of course our daughter Evelyn is the proverbial icing on the cake.

Conclusion

These two accounts have taught me some very important things about the way God speaks. First, God has his own timetable for unfolding his plan in our lives and we need to allow that timetable to play out. Second, God will move heaven and earth to answer our prayers, especially when we yield ourselves to him and his will. God literally changed the flight schedule of my friend and his wife so that I could have someone to eat lunch with and so that God could use the event to speak direction into my life. Third, God does in fact do exceedingly and abundantly above all we could ever ask or think (Eph 3:20). What I felt was the way God's word *should* be fulfilled was so much less effective than the perfect plan of God. Fourth, as believers we need to be alert to the voice of God in our lives. Sometimes it is audible, and sometimes it is a strong inclination or impression upon one's life. At other times it is being alert to the still small voice of God that says, "this is the way to go, walk ye in it" (Isa 30:21).

Chapter 12

God Speaks through Answered Prayer

IT GOES WITHOUT SAYING that prayer is speaking to God. And God's responses to our prayers are his way of speaking to us. Not surprisingly, sometimes when God answers our prayers we refuse to believe it is actually happening. I think of the events recorded in Acts 12. After Herod arrested Peter, the early church prayed for his release from prison (Acts 12:5). God answered their prayers by miraculously sending an angel to remove Peter's chains and open the doors of the prison allowing Peter to escape. Peter went to the home of Mary, the mother of Mark, but the people inside the house refused to believe it was true until they saw Peter (Acts 12:14–16). At the same time, the Bible is replete with examples of people praying and God answering those prayers as expected by the supplicant. Moses is a prime example of this, especially when he prayed that God would end each of the plagues against Egypt (Exod 8:12–13, 29–31; 9:28–33; 10:18–19; cf. Num 11:2). At other times God answers prayers in very unique ways. When Daniel prayed about Jeremiah's seventy weeks his prayer is answered by none other than Gabriel (9:20–27). At other times, answers to our prayers do not come when we expect it. Again, Daniel comes to mind. The answer to his prayer in Daniel 10 did not come in the expected timeframe. It was delayed for three weeks by demonic forces (10:13), but ultimately reached Daniel (10:9–14). While I may not have experienced all of these scenarios, one of the things that I have learned throughout my life is that God does answer prayer. When he does that, God speaks to us.

God Can Speak Immediately by Answering Prayer

As just noted, learning how God speaks through prayer is a process that can take a lifetime. Nevertheless, when God does answer one's prayers, trust in the God-human relationship grows. Perhaps one of the most memorable times when God answered my prayer was also one of the most miraculous.

Before starting Bible school, I was a musician in our church band. Every week prior to the service we would all meet in the prayer room and pray that God would use us as we ministered in music. On one of these nights I was particularly troubled about things that had been going on in my life. Some of the people in my church had been talking about me behind my back, especially as it related to things in my past. I knew that God had forgiven me of many things but I found it particularly hard to move on from them because people would not stop bringing them up and talking about them amongst themselves. Some might have felt I was being too sensitive, but the truth was, it was affecting my ability to trust people and it certainly did not promote church unity. I had even come to the place where I began to question if I actually *did* deserve the treatment I was receiving. Perhaps God was in fact displeased with me and had not forgiven me of everything. On that particular Sunday, these concerns had come to a head. I took these things to God in prayer before the service that night and pleaded for God to answer my prayer and speak to me. Were the people right or was God? I can recall that this was one of those occasions when I was desperate before God. I was hurting and I needed an answer *sooner* rather than later.

I finished my prayer and took my place at the drums, which were off to one side of the platform. When the music began I tried to take my mind off what I had prayed but I found it next to impossible to get my thoughts to switch from that subject to my task at hand. I tried to put on a brave face but I am sure the anguish in my heart was evident in my countenance. Fortunately I had enough drums and cymbals around me to hide my emotions and expressions from searching eyes. Looking back at it now, however, I can say that the words of the psalmist ring true: "Where can I go to escape your Spirit? Where can I flee to escape your presence? If I ascend to heaven, you are there. If I lay down in Sheol, behold you are there. If I am carried on the wings of the dawn or if I dwell by the distant sea even there your hand will lead me and your right hand will hold me" (Ps 139:7-10; my translation).

At about the mid-point of the service, as the pastor was leading in singing, the door of the church opened and a man walked into the foyer. Our church at that time was relatively small, seating about 200 people, although we had about 80 on a regular week. From where I sat on the drums I could see clearly all the way into the foyer, especially when the swinging doors, which separated the foyer from the main sanctuary, were open. The man that came in was dressed in what I would describe as a very "festive" shirt, blue jeans, and cowboy boots. Even though we lived in the country, this kind of attire was not the norm for anyone from my area. Much to my surprise, the pastor, who remember was leading the singing, left the platform and walked down to the man and warmly greeted him. After just a few seconds of conversation the man followed our pastor down the church aisle and right up onto the stage. I had never seen this man before. I could not imagine what was going on. All of my thoughts about what I had prayed slipped away as I now became fixated on what had just happened. What an odd thing. In the middle of a service a complete stranger, at least to most everyone except the pastor that is, walks into the church and now is sitting on the stage just a few feet from my drum set.

When the worship service ended I walked off the stage and took a seat in the front row of the church. On that particular night I sat completely by myself in the row. Although a few people were sitting in the row directly behind me, there was nothing shielding me from the sight of the speaker. I quickly realized that this was perhaps not the best idea.

God Speaks through Answered Prayer

Our pastor approached the pulpit and proceeded to introduce our "visitor" as a pastor friend from Massachusetts. Apparently he had been in town visiting his parents while he was on vacation when, on a whim, he decided to stop by our church—this of course not only explained why he walked in late, but it also accounted for the casual "out of town" attire. I found the introduction helpful in explaining my earlier consternation but what happened next perplexed me. The pastor then proceeded to say that he had just asked his friend to preach to us. I thought that this was strange. Who would be ready to preach on the spur of the moment? Later, after going to Bible school, I realized that in ministry there is an old saying, "Be ready at a moment's notice to preach, give a testimony, or to die."

The gentleman approached the pulpit in his festive shirt and cowboy boots and looked out at the congregation and read his text. Although I cannot recall the exact details of it I do recall that the sermon points hit on the very things that I had been concerned about in my life. As the preacher moved from one point to the next, he hit ever closer to home with the things I had been praying about. I wept uncontrollably as I realized that God was answering my prayer, which I had prayed before the service. The harder the preacher preached the more emotional I became. I am sure I attracted his attention but I could not control what the Spirit was doing in my life. At one point the speaker looked out at the audience and he said, "There are people in here that God has forgiven much. God wants you to know that he has thrown those sins into the sea (cf. Micah 7:19) and he has put up 'no fishing' signs around that sea. However, there are others of you who have dared to go fishing in that pond by bringing up the past sins of others. God is telling you to stop that!" At that point I knew that God had brought this man to answer my prayer. He spoke to the very thing I had prayed about before the service.

After the service was over the special speaker came down and laid his hand on me and prayed that God would work in my life. Of course he had no idea what I had prayed or that God had used him in a very meaningful way to answer my prayer. Again

I thought of what had just transpired. What are the odds that a complete stranger, on a whim, would drop by my church, in a different country mind you, and deliver an unexpected sermon that spoke directly to what I had been praying about? And what are the odds that my home pastor would actually ask him to speak on the spur of the moment? God is not a God of "coincidences." That is the type of God that I serve. He can use others to speak to me and he does it by hearing and answering my prayers when I am in a desperate place.

Several years later I met that preacher again. I was visiting the church of a friend in Massachusetts, and you guessed it, it was the home church of the special speaker who had visited my church from years prior. I told my friend what had happened several years earlier. She insisted that I tell her pastor. When she got his attention after the service he came up to me and I told him about how he had ministered to me and how God had used him to answer my prayer. He said he remembered the night and thanked me. We rejoiced in God's goodness and in the fact that God had used him in this special way.

Conclusion

While I took more space than normal to relate the account above, the reason I did so was to point out how much God loves his children and to show to what extent he will go to answer our prayers. Now that is not to say that he has answered every prayer in a similar fashion and in that short of a time frame (see more below), but it does prove that when we are in desperate need of God's help he is there, for indeed, the fervent prayer of a righteous man or woman is effective (James 5:16).

Chapter 13

God Speaks through the Silence of Unanswered Prayer

A COMMON REFRAIN AMONG believers is that God has a perfect plan for our lives. Numerous times I have heard Christians quote either Mark 11:24, "Therefore I say to you, all things for which you pray and ask, believe that you have received them, and they shall be *granted* you" (NASB), or Jeremiah 29:11, "For I know the thoughts that I think toward you, saith the LORD, thoughts of peace, and not of evil, to give you an expected end" (KJV). These are very encouraging verses to be sure, but more often than not, God does not answer our prayers in the time frame that we expect and in some cases, good things do not happen to us even when we pray. Indeed, how should you respond when you do not see good things happening even though you have followed all the "rules"? Do we really believe deep down that God hears and answers prayer and has only good things for our future, especially when it relates to our own lives? While my readers may think that I have an "inside connection" to the Almighty based upon what I have written in this book, at times this conclusion seems to be far from the actual facts on the ground. The truth is we all have periods of doubt and questioning, even when we have witnessed firsthand God speaking to us through various means. Consider John the Baptist's low point when he was in prison. Even though he knew that Jesus was the one to come (John 1:29–35), he still questioned if Jesus was the Messiah when he was faced with death and the depressing status of being the prisoner of Herod (Matt 11:2–5; Luke 7:18–20).

We are all human, and in the midst of trials, past answers do not always serve as comfort in the midst of present pain and turmoil. True, we can draw on what God has done. And, yes, there is a level of trust that develops in our relationship with God over time. But we still like to hear from him when we pray, especially for the big decisions of life. The account that follows is a clear example of what happened in my life when God did not speak or answer my prayer in what I felt was a timely fashion or in the way I thought was best. Spoiler alert: hindsight is always 20/20. God had a perfect plan; I just needed to trust him.

Praying for a Job

Thus far I have given a number of details about the process of God calling me and helping me to get through my thirteen years of schooling and four degrees in Bible. Towards the end of my educational path, I began to start the job search process. For a long time I felt that God was calling me back to my undergraduate school to be a teacher. However, as time went on I could see that God was closing that door. I began to seek his will and apply for teaching positions in my final two years of PhD studies. Beginning in 2007 I answered job search postings that I felt were a pretty good fit for my training and ecclesiological bent. One by one the rejection letters returned. At first I was not overly concerned; I had always felt that God would open the door he wanted me to walk through and I still had my dissertation to complete so I had some time. By the end of 2007 and the beginning of 2008 I stepped up the job search process because my planned graduation date was quickly approaching in 2009. I had also started to date a lady who would eventually become my wife. I needed security moving forward if I was going to get married and start a family. One after another I received more and more rejection letters. Even schools at which I thought I would make a good candidate rejected my applications.

God Speaks through the Silence of Unanswered Prayer

As the stack of rejection letters started to grow, my wedding date in August of 2008 was quickly approaching. I went home in the summer of 2008 and worked as a carpenter to pay for my last year of schooling and to set aside some money for my upcoming wedding and to prepare for the costs of married life. I returned to Toronto in the fall of 2008—now a married student—to finish my last year of PhD work. All I had remaining was to complete some final revisions on my dissertation. Of course, everyone now knows about the financial disaster that hit the financial markets during the fall of 2008. Up until this point I was somewhat uncertain of what God was doing in my life when it came to finding a job. After the financial crash of September 2008, however, I really began to get nervous (again, I am human). Where job-posting websites previously listed dozens of available jobs in Old Testament and Hebrew Bible, almost overnight most of those job postings disappeared as universities and institutions of higher education scrambled to stop the financial bleeding. I will admit that I was beginning to get concerned. How was God going to fix this mess and get me a job?

I was now starting to think more globally in my job search. I felt that if I could just be given a chance to interview, with the help of God, I could "wow" the interviewers and secure a job (as I will point out below, God has a sense of humor in this regard). In the spring of 2009, I was chosen as one of three final candidates to interview for a job in London, England. My wife and I flew to London and after the interview I was asked if I wanted the job. I answered in the affirmative and was instructed by the principal of the school to write a letter of intent as to why I wanted to teach at the school. A few days later my wife and I flew back to Toronto, Canada under the assumption that it would be just a matter of days for the school to go through the formalities of confirming the job offering and sending us the particulars. Being so far from our homes and families would not be an ideal situation for sure, but if this was where God wanted us then we were ready to go.

As we waited the days quickly turned into weeks. I finally sent an email asking about the status of the job. The principal apologetically responded telling me that they had decided not to offer any of the candidates a full-time position. I had felt like I was on a roller-coaster emotionally. Now the ride had come to a screeching halt. To add insult to injury, a couple of my fellow students had already been offered positions *before* they had even started their dissertations. And here I was, now down to the final stages of my program and getting ready to defend my thesis in the fall, with not one job prospect on the horizon!

Although I had been praying in earnest for some time about a job, I now took it to the next level. I can remember leaving the apartment one night and walking into the partially enclosed outdoor courtyard at Wycliffe College and "having it out" with God. I prayed intensely. I reminded God that I had done everything I knew to do. I had remained faithful to the Bible despite the constant pressure from more minimalist professors for me to compromise how I believe and teach the Bible. I can remember lifting my voice to God and asking him what he was doing in my life. All I heard was silence! I walked back into the apartment and kept my prayer to myself.

A few days later my wife came to me and said, "I feel like God is wanting us to go and do some short-term missions work in the Gambia, West Africa." A mutual friend of ours operated a non-profit ministry to the predominantly Muslim country and was looking for teachers to go and teach intensive classes in the Bible at a new Bible school. My immediate response when he had asked me earlier was a flat out, No! The last place I wanted to go was to Africa. I needed my running water, electricity, and comfortable bed. Once again, obviously God has a sense of humor. The circumstances reminded me of a popular song I had heard back in the 90s titled, "Please Don't Send Me to Africa" by Scott Wesley Brown. However, now I began to consider this possibility. After all, God had closed every other door.

My wife and I agreed to do a five week stint in the Gambia, and also started planning to do a two-week archaeological dig in Israel after completing our teaching assignments in Africa. We thought that while we were half-way around the world we might just as well take the opportunity to travel on to Israel and do an

God Speaks through the Silence of Unanswered Prayer

archaeological dig, something we both had dreamed about doing. It also was very cost effective seeing how we only had to get flights from Brussels, Belgium as opposed to having to fly from Toronto, Canada. At the time I did not know what God was doing in my life, but I felt that this was the door that was opening so I walked through it. I would soon realize that God had everything planned out better than I could possibly imagine.

After arriving in the Gambia, my wife and I went to work putting the final touches on our lectures and getting ready to teach our classes. I also started pulling together some of my thoughts for a possible book idea. That preliminary work would develop into one of my more popular books—*John's Use of Ezekiel*— which I wrote in 2015. My time in Africa was relaxing as I gathered my thoughts and spent time in prayer seeking God's direction. Interestingly, it was during my time in the Gambia that I received an email that would change my life. One of my professors, whom I had studied under during my PhD program, Dr. Marion Taylor, sent me a job posting and said she thought it would be a good fit for me. Here I was not even looking for a job at the moment and God used her to send me a job posting for a position back in Alberta, Canada!

I filled out the job application and sent my information to the school via email. The school was looking to fill the position for the fall and here it was already early May. A few days later the representative for the school responded and asked if they could set up a phone interview. In Africa, this is questionable at best. I agreed but told them we may have to do a Skype interview instead because the phone service was too spotty. On the appointed day we had the interview and they followed it up with an offer for an on-campus interview when I got back from my travels in Africa and Israel in early June. I agreed.

My wife and I completed our teaching contract in the Gambia and flew on to Israel to do our archaeological dig. Little did I know that that two-week volunteer dig would open up another opportunity that has been a part of my life even to this day. When my wife searched for a dig in which for us to participate, we had no idea which one to choose. There were multiple digs going on at the same time throughout Israel. We made the decision to join a dig sponsored by the Associates for Biblical Research solely on the basis of the fact that the dig location was the Old Testament site of Joshua's Ai, my area of research and study. It was later that we found out that the dig we went on was one of the few digs in Israel whose leadership has an evangelical and conservative ideology; a perfect fit for us. Since that first archaeological experience I have joined the organization responsible for the dig and have participated in nine seasons. I am now a field archaeologist with the group and have made amazing friendships in Canada, the US, and Israel.

Returning from the dig, my wife and I flew directly to Alberta, Canada from Israel. Accounting for the time difference, I went into the interview with nine hours of jet lag. I had also lost a lot of weight in Africa because of the changed diet and sickness due to my malaria medication. Moreover, I had just completed two weeks of heavy manual labor in Israel. To put it simply, I was a mess. Due to lack of sleep and fatigue, at one point during the job interview I was so emotional when answering one of their questions that my wife had to finish answering the question for me! I had certainly not "wowed" anyone on that day. I left the interview thinking there was no way I would ever be given the job. But in the midst of my weakness, God was merciful and had other ideas. Much to my surprise, I was offered the position before I returned home. While the remuneration was an extreme pay cut from what I was used to as a carpenter I felt that this was where I needed to be at that juncture in my life. Many years earlier I had told God that money was not the issue; I wanted to work for him. For that reason, I accepted the position.

To recap: in the midst of an economic downturn, and with a stack of rejection letters on my desk, God gave me a job! Looking back I feel that God had wanted me to yield my will to his, even though I thought I already had done so. When I submitted my will to his and went to Africa to minister—even though it was for only five weeks—God gave me my first job. God used my wife to prompt me in that direction. Through my willingness to go, God had also opened the door for me to do archaeology. This field of study has improved my teaching and has opened doors for speaking and publishing that I would never have had otherwise. To this day, I take students to Israel every year to experience getting their hands "dirty" in the Bible.

The Continuing Unfolding Plan of God

The next few months of my life were a whirlwind; I had to collect all my material possessions together, put them all in a U-Haul van, move across Canada, settle into a new apartment, start my new job, and prepare new classes. I can remember that at one point, as Christine and I traveled across Canada, my wife starting to realize the gravity of the move. With this move we were over a five-day journey by car from our families! She began to cry. I asked her if everything was okay and she said to me that she knew we were probably going to be in Alberta for a very long time. She said she knew that when I said I was going to do something I was committed to doing it. I looked at her and reminded her that we did not know the future and what God had in store for us. I would realize later just how prophetic that statement was.

As I set to work preparing my new classes for the fall, I was excited at this new stage in my life. That excitement quickly changed to one of concern when the president of the school called an emergency meeting for all the faculty and staff of the institution just a few days prior to the beginning of the semester. He said that the school was experiencing financial difficulties and that if they continued, the chances of the school remaining open would be slim.

You can imagine how that announcement made me feel. Prior to moving all the way across the country, I had specifically asked the dean of the school if the institution was financially solvent, and he had said yes! Had I missed the voice of God? When I told my wife the news we immediately began to ask for God's direction. I came from a place in my life as a carpenter where I was used to having financial stability. We both felt that we needed to pray, but that also I should begin the job hunt again. On this latter point we both had peace.

It was disconcerting to think about the prospects of packing up once again and moving after just a few months. Nevertheless, I started looking for work again in the early fall of that same year. Immediately, I came across a posting for an Old Testament professor in Cleveland, Tennessee at Lee University. I was unfamiliar with Lee University even though I realized later that I had driven by the school on numerous occasions when I was doing my master's work at Beeson Divinity School. I emailed the chair of the department and asked if there was any way I could meet one of the faculty while I was at the Society of Biblical Literature annual meeting in Atlanta, Georgia. The department chair said there was going to be at least one person there and that I could meet him. Little did I know that that person would later become one of my best friends, a mentor, and a confidant.

When I met Dr. Bill Simmons in November of 2010, based upon what he said, I felt that Lee was a good fit, especially with its Pentecostal history. I went ahead and applied to the school and in mid-February I had a phone interview. Not long afterwards, they extended an invitation to me to do an on-campus interview in early April. Over the next few weeks I set aside some time for prayer and fasting as I asked God to open or close this door. As I had often done in the past, this was the way I had asked God to speak to me. A few weeks after the on-campus interview, I was offered the position, which I saw as confirmation from God that I was to take the job offer. It had indeed been a whirlwind but I knew that my position at Lee University was where God had intended for me to be all along.

Now some might be saying that I had thought my first job position was "God's will." Why would God change his mind so quickly? The reality is that there is no doubt in my mind that it was God's will for me to be at that first job if only for one year. What I did not realize until later is that Lee University was looking for someone with teaching experience. Teaching a full slate of courses at my previous school had allowed me to gain a level of experience in the classroom, which they had been looking for. Also, the teaching load at my previous school was relatively light and as such had allowed me plenty of time to prepare my classes and lectures for the four major blocks of the Old Testament (Pentateuch, Historical Books, Wisdom Literature, and the Prophets). These preps enabled me to step into my new position prepared to teach almost any class in the Old Testament. Amazingly enough, three of the main upper-level classes that I was asked to teach were three of the four I had already prepared.

From the time I had started my initial job search in 2007 until I landed the job that God had prepared for me it had been a total of four years. In that time I had many days and weeks of not knowing what God was doing. Indeed, many times I felt that his silence was deafening. I had questioned what he was doing on more than one occasion. Yet, had God told me up front that I had to wait for four years to get the perfect job I may have grown impatient and faltered in my faith. The truth is that I had remained busy working for God the whole time during those four years. I never was without a paid position of some sort. And looking back he opened so many doors for me that I could not begin to imagine how I could have made it any better.

As I drove with my very pregnant wife in another U-Haul across the US to my new job, I looked over to her and reminded her of our previous journey a year earlier across Canada when she had wept thinking that we would be in western Canada away from family for the rest of our lives. I encouraged her once again that God had a plan; one that was good and one that gave us a future and a hope.

Conclusion

Knowing the will of God is good, but allowing him to speak to you through silent trust is what has caused me to grow in my faith even more. Yes, hindsight is 20/20. It reminds me of the famous poem footprints in the sand. My God had carried me along even when I did not know he was working behind the scenes to orchestrate the perfect plan for my life. Was it always easy? Of course, it was not. Was it worth it? Absolutely!

Chapter 14

God Speaks through His Miraculous Protection

THROUGHOUT THE BIBLE GOD often spoke to his people through miracles. In many ways these miraculous events spoke to the people about who God is. The plagues against Egypt were performed not just to convince the Pharaoh and the Egyptians to let the children of Israel leave Egypt, they were also done so that the Egyptians and Israel would know that Yahweh was in fact God (Exod 6:7; 7:5, 17; 8:22; 10:2; 14:4, 18; 16:12; 29:46; 31:13). In the book of Ezekiel, the idea of Israel learning about who their God was by means of a re-education process is a predominant theme. Indeed, no less than 63 times, Ezekiel records the statement that Israel "would know" who God was through his acts and miraculous interventions. Not surprisingly, throughout the Gospels, especially in the book of John, Jesus performs miracles to convince the people of Israel who he is: the Son of God. Thus, it becomes evident that God's use of the miraculous was a means of God breaking into human existence and speaking to his people in a very special way: the miraculous shouts out the fact that God is the one true God.

In biblical times, God's protection, many times through a miraculous event, proved to the people of God that he was with them, and by extension, was speaking to them. Often times, later a particular leader would look back at those events and interpret them as God-ordained. A good example of this type of introspection can be seen in how David assessed God's working in his life to protect him. There are a number of cases in 1 and 2 Samuel and the Psalms where this happens. For example, when David ran from Saul and went to Achish in the land of the Philistines, David feared for his life when the Philistines recognized him as the man who had killed so many of them in the past. David feigned insanity and escaped from danger (1 Sam 21:10—22:1). Later, however, when he wrote a psalm reflecting on that past event, he credited his escape to the intervention of God (Psalms 34 and 56). What changed? Was God there in the original event or was David merely spiritualizing it later? It seems more likely that David looked back on these miraculous events and began to see the hand of God working throughout his life. Indeed, these were not mere coincidences but rather the working of God in his life to protect and guide him.

On the other hand, sometimes you can recognize God's working in a situation almost immediately with virtually no lag time between the event and our spontaneous thanksgiving to God. In the Bible we see this play out in a number of situations. Two are found in Exodus and Judges. In Exodus Moses and Miriam write and sing the Song of the Sea in Exodus 15 immediately after the defeat of Pharaoh and his army recorded in chapter 14. In Judges 5, Deborah and Barak sing a song of praise to Yahweh after their defeat of Sisera and his hoards noted in chapter 4. They identify the natural phenomenon of a severe rain storm as God's handiwork (Judg 5:20-21; cf. Josh 10:11). While it is true that in these situations God's actions are a form of non-verbal communication, the biblical writers certainly understood these events as issuing from God. In these situations it is clear that God is, nonetheless, speaking to his people. He is telling them that he is with them; that he is for them, and that they can trust him. Indeed, through these events the leaders of Israel were assured that God spoke to them in the first place to go into battle or to cross the Red Sea (although this latter case already involved a divine intervention through miraculous means).

God Speaks through His Miraculous Protection

In light of these types of events in the Bible, one of the ways that I have experienced God's voice in my life has been through his miraculous protection. These experiences of God's protection have spoken to me and have shown me that God has a special plan for my life even though the Enemy has tried very hard to end my life on more than one occasion. I want to share three different events that all took place prior to God opening the door for me to do ministry. Looking back on these events and God's miraculous protection, I can tell that God was speaking to me even though I may not have understood exactly what he was saying.

God's Protection on the Highway

God has protected me so many times while driving that I hardly know where to begin. Having owned a number of motorcycles alone required God to send his guardian angels to my aid on more than one occasion. My wife is very happy with the fact that my motorcycling passion has long since passed. Apart from the numerous situations where God protected me during my motorcycling days from the time I was in grade nine until my early twenties, one divine act related to my early days driving a car stands out as particularly memorable.

Not too long after I purchased my second car, a Toyota Tercel, in the late 1980s I was miraculously protected by the hand of God. Having grown up in New Brunswick, Canada snow was a common occurrence and something I had learned to drive on from the time I was sixteen. What I had not had much experience with, however, was operating a front-wheel-drive vehicle in snow. This is an experience completely different than driving a rear-wheel-drive car in the snow.

One night I was on my way to a hockey game and was driving a bit too fast for the road conditions. I was on the main provincial road known as the Trans-Canada Highway, which ran on the outskirts of our town. Even though it was the main thoroughfare in Canada, in our area of the province, the highway handled two-way traffic as opposed to being a divided highway. That particular night

89

the weather had been inclement and the roads were covered with a heavy slushy snow. When I came to a gradual turn in the highway, I could feel my car starting to fishtail. On this same turn in the road was the entrance to one of the largest trucking companies in our province. As such, transport trucks with their trailers were constantly coming and going from the depot. As I began to lose control I immediately thought of the possibilities of trucks coming in the opposite direction. Within seconds my car spun around in the road and I found myself driving backwards down the opposite side of the road into oncoming traffic as I headed for the ditch. Braking did little to slow the car down on the slush-covered road. I braced for impact with either a truck or the ditch, whichever came first. Fortunately, I went into the ditch first. I still was not out of trouble though because I was still moving fairly fast. The snow-filled ditch began to slow my car down marginally. Then, with a bang, the rear end of my car hit a culvert in a driveway and threw my car into the air causing the car to rotate 90 degrees and land perfectly on a driveway. My car, although now stopped, had stalled out.

I got out of the vehicle to inspect the damage. Instead of finding a mangled tail end of the car, I found that the only thing wrong with my car was that some mud had been driven up into the tail pipe. I took one of my drumsticks from the car and cleaned it out. The car started and ran perfectly. I slowly made my way to the hockey game, slightly shaken up but nonetheless okay.

While some may just say that I was lucky, several "coincidences" had to happen at the same time for me to have averted disaster. First, God had protected me from trucks and cars as I slid down the road backwards into oncoming traffic. No sooner had my car come to rest on the driveway then a truck passed on the highway. Second, by hitting the rear end of the car on the edge of the culvert, I was protected from putting my head through the windshield (this was before mandatory airbags and seatbelts). I walked away with no injuries. Third, no damage happened to my car because the heavy snow in the ditch cushioned much of the impact when I left the road.

God Speaks through His Miraculous Protection

At the time I did not think too much about the accident, but now that I look back at the numerous times God protected me I am convinced that this was just one more time when the Enemy had tried to end my life when I was younger. This was especially true considering the occupation I had chosen.

God's Protection at Work

Choosing carpentry as an occupation meant that on a daily basis I was at risk of serious injury or even death. I cannot count the number of times God protected me. Again, a couple of incidents when God saved me from death stand out above all the rest.

It was the fall of 1987 and I was working with my two brothers on a large potato storage and packing building. An older building was attached to the new structure on the north end. We were at the point of putting the steel roofing on the new building when disaster happened. One morning in October we arrived bright and early to go to work but due to the heavy frost we could not work on the frosty steel roof. However, some of our electrical cords were still on the roof from the previous day. I decided to go up and bring them down off the roof so we could work on other projects until the frost melted in the morning sun. I had every intention on being careful. I had quickly looked at the roof and had seen that the sun had already melted the frost on the eastern slope. We were actually using the roof of the older building, which was attached to the new structure on the north, to climb on up to the taller new structure. Unfortunately, what I had failed to take note of was that the shaded part of the old building attached on the north end of the taller new structure had an extra amount of frost covering it, which the sun had not melted yet.

When I stepped onto the old roof near its peak, I immediately lost my footing and slipped on the wet frosty steel. I fell onto my knees and began to slide backwards down the roof. No matter how hard I tried to stop my sliding, I only increased in speed. Although the old roof was only about 18 feet off the ground, directly below where I was falling we had just recently excavated a large hole for the new sewage system. This hole added an extra three or four feet to the distance I had to fall. The new steel sewage tank was already installed in the hole but remained uncovered. On one side of the tank, closest to the old building, a large four-foot round boulder lay exposed. As I shot over the edge of the roof backwards I looked over my shoulder and saw the boulder quickly approaching. Fortunately, I was falling feet first. I landed with both feet on top of the boulder but my head and upper body continued their momentum downward between my legs. My head hit the rock between my feet and then bounced off the rock and thrust my upper body upwards as I fell backwards down into the hole on top of the sewage tank. There I sat as a yelled for help.

A short time later an ambulance arrived but I was already starting to go into shock. By the time the ambulance arrived at the hospital I was stabilized. X-rays revealed that I had broken three metatarsals in my right foot. The doctor was concerned about a head injury because I had lost a good portion of the skin on one side of my head when I hit the rock. The doctors said I was very lucky to be alive. I knew that God had once again protected me. Within two and a half weeks I was back at work.

The second event took place in the early 90s. I was helping a friend clean his chimney on a two-story house in the middle of the winter. He had already placed one tall ladder up against the house so that the top of the ladder rested on the edge of the roof at the eve line. I had to carry a second aluminum ladder with a hook on its top up the first ladder and slide it up the steep-pitched roof and hook it on the ridge. As I reached the top of the first ladder I pulled the second ladder up and laid it on the roof sloop above me. All I needed to do was to push the second ladder up the slope until the hook dropped over the ridge. As I was giving the second ladder one last push up the slope, the bottom of the ladder I was standing on slipped out at the base and fell causing me to let go of the ladder I was pushing up the slope. I fell down the side of the house and landed between the rungs of the first ladder in a large snowbank beside the house. Unfortunately, I had not gotten the second ladder that was laying on the slope of the roof hooked

God Speaks through His Miraculous Protection

over the ridge. Due to this fact, the second ladder proceeded to slip down the slope and fall down the side of the house as well. It all happened so fast. Because I was wedged between the rungs of the first ladder with my feet firmly stuck in the snowbank, all I could do was put my head down and hope for the best. The second aluminum ladder struck me on the brim of my ball cap and cut through the brim and lodged in the skin of my forehead. I bled profusely and started to go into shock. My friend rushed me to the hospital where I received multiple stiches in my forehead. Again, the doctor said I was lucky to be alive.

Later I assessed what had actually happened that morning. I always check the base of my ladders to make sure they are secure on the ground. When I checked the base of the ladder that day I thought it was sitting on the bare ground. I did not realize that my friend had just thrown down some ashes over the ice on which the ladder was sitting. This made the ice look like sandy soil. The other thing I noticed is that on that particular morning I had put on a new cap because it was heavier and warmer than my normal hat. The brim of that cap had an extra thick hard plastic lining under the fabric on the brim. It was that extra thickness that had acted like a hard hat to blunt the force of the ladder and to stop the sharp metal leg of the ladder from piercing my skull, which it easily would have done had I not been wearing that hat. I had never had a hat like before or since (what are the odds!). To this day I have a scar that reminds me of God's protection.

Some might say I was clumsy and careless, and I guess in my haste that is a fair analysis. Nevertheless, in both of these cases God protected me from very serious head injuries. I know that through these events God was not only protecting me, he was also speaking to me. He was telling me that he had a plan for my life and that it was not yet my time to die. God is indeed good. When I consider all the ways he has protected me during my years as a carpenter I cannot thank him enough. Shortly after these two near-death experiences, I began to pray a special prayer anytime I was in a potentially dangerous situation. I always prayed, "Dear God give me your protection and make my feet firm. Please keep me from falling or hurting myself. Amen." Looking back now, I see that God was teaching me the value of prayer and the importance of giving him thanks for all the ways he protects especially those that we take for granted on a daily basis.

Conclusion

What all of these miraculous events of protection have taught me is that God uses a variety of means to speak to his children. Many times we may simply thank God for his protection without really considering what he is *saying* to us through the experience. It is in the midst of these close encounters with death that God sometimes speaks the clearest. For me it was coming to an understanding that God had a special purpose for my life. Of course God's "voice" in these matters became clear only later when I looked back and began to assess how he had worked miraculously to protect me. To be sure, Christians constantly need to assess and reassess our lives to gain a real appreciation for all that God does and how he is speaking to us.

Chapter 15

God Speaks through His Acts of Healing

I HAVE RESERVED THE category of healing to the last because of the sometimes troubling nature of the topic. My hope is that by demonstrating throughout the earlier chapters of this book the numerous other ways that God speaks, perhaps we should not be so quick to place undue weight on this one area of God's working power, especially when he may not extend a healing touch to us or our loved ones. To be sure, the reason that healing is a troubling topic for many is due to the fact that many times God in fact does not heal when we ask for it. As such, people tend to come to the conclusion that God does not speak to us or care about us, and in some extreme cases people reach the conclusion that if God will not listen to their prayers for healing then maybe he does not exist at all. Sadly, some believers depart the faith because of the lack of God's intervention in healing a loved one or even themselves.

Now certainly receiving a healing is a very tangible way to sense that God cares and is speaking to us; however, that does not mean that he will *always* do so. The Bible records examples where God did not heal even some of his most beloved disciples and followers. Paul's prayer to be delivered of the thorn in his side (2 Cor 12:7–9) comes to mind as does David's prayer for God to heal his son after his affair with Bathsheba (2 Samuel 12). And even Jesus did not do many miracles in his home town because of their lack of faith (Matt 13:58). From a personal perspective I have experienced God's apparent refusal to answer prayers for healing. My mother, brother-in-law, and my best friend all died from cancer. I have colleagues who have lost loved ones to this disease despite countless prayers for healing. Why did God not heal in these cases? I know I did everything I knew to do from a biblical perspective. Perhaps I will never know why God did not act in these situations this side of eternity. Maybe in some cases God's healing is only intended for some when they reach eternity. What is important to remember is that just because someone does not get healed this side of heaven does not mean that God does not heal at all or that he does not speak. Again, the Bible is filled with examples of the healing power of God. I would like to relate three times when God has performed what I would classify as a clear healing touch in my body or the body of someone close to me.

The Faith of a Child

One of my earliest remembrances of how God treats his children is God's healing of my knees as a boy. I cannot recall the exact date, but when I was going through my rapid growth spurts my knees would hurt so badly that in some cases I would cry myself to sleep. One night when I was having a particular bout with severe pain I remember praying to God for a touch in my body. Shortly thereafter I fell asleep and had a good night's sleep. Not long afterwards I noticed that I had not had pain in my legs since that night. I recall looking at my knees that had given me so much pain in the past and something was different. On the inside of my knees on exactly the same place on both legs there was a short inch-and-a-half-long scar. I had never noticed these scars before that day. They were not obvious like some of the scars I had acquired in the past. As I stared at them I felt God impressing upon me that he had "operated" on them and fixed the problem.

Now I am sure that many will say that God does not need to "operate" in order to heal someone. While this is indeed true, that

God Speaks through His Acts of Healing

does not mean God cannot use this method for a greater purpose. God's fashioning of Eve after performing "surgery" on Adam is a perfect example of just such a case (Gen 2:21–22). For me the scars were a visible sign at a young age that God had heard me and that he answers prayer. All I know is that I have never had a knee ache since that night!

Why did God heal in that situation? Maybe it was the childlike faith I had. I know that even today when I pray for needs in my family I will sometimes call my children around me or my wife and have them pray. Others might still be skeptical that I was but a child and that this event was just one time. The truth is God has performed a number of healings in my life since that one experience back when I was a child.

The Prayer of Desperation

One of the more memorable times when I know God intervened and healed my body was in the fall of 1995. During the early 90s I took up bodybuilding at my local gym. Because I did not believe in using steroids or other body enhancing chemicals, I used natural foods to supplement my diet and make up for the expended calories I was using every day in the gym. Part of my diet regimen was tuna fish and the addition of raw eggs to my milkshakes. After a couple years of working out I had gained almost twenty-five pounds of muscle and I felt great. It was not a rapid weight-gain program for sure, but as a carpenter doing physical activity all day, I did see muscle-mass gains during this time.

In the fall of 1995, I took on a project to build a medium sized log home in my local town. The new house was not too far from my gym. I would work all day on the home and then drive over to the gym after work. Within the first couple weeks of the project I started feeling sickly with severe abdominal pains. Over a period of days I went from eating four or five big meals a day to eating only half of a sandwich at a time, if I could eat food at all. Anytime I did try to eat I would immediately get severe abdominal cramps that would put me into the fetal position in pain for over an hour or more. This went on for about two weeks as I continued to work during the day lifting and setting into place large logs and driving twelve-inch spikes with a sledgehammer to secure them in place. I was in a weakened state during most of that time. After the first few days of the symptoms, I went to the local hospital and had numerous tests run but they could not find anything wrong with my digestive system. The doctors said it would pass; however, the pain did not go away, it only got worse. Of course the sickness had forced me to take a break from bodybuilding and the diet that went along with it.

One night about a week later after eating a small supper I found myself once again laying on the upstairs floor of my home in such pain I could hardly stand it. I had come to the end of my proverbial rope. I called out to God for help and asked him to heal me of this extreme pain. I was also concerned about my physical health. Being unable to eat regular meals, yet still having to work as a carpenter because I was self-employed, I could see that I was losing weight at a rapid pace as my fat stores quickly were depleted. As I lay on the floor I called to my mom, dad, and sister and pleaded with them to take me to the major provincial hospital about an hour and a half away from home. I no longer had any faith in the local hospital to diagnose the problem.

When I arrived at the hospital I was still suffering the effects of the small meal I had eaten over two hours earlier. The doctors immediately put me on fluids intravenously to hydrate me as they tried to stabilize me. It was one of the few times I had ever been in the hospital overnight. In my state of desperation, I prayed a lot that night and found out later that a lot of other people from my church were praying too. I drifted in and out of sleep all that night as I prayed for healing in my body. When I finally came to early the next morning I sat up in bed perfectly fine! I got up, checked myself out, and called for someone to take me home.

Although I was weak, my stomach felt fine. Within a couple of days of slowly restarting my digestive system and eating regular meals I was back to normal. The doctors never did figure out what had been my problem or how I had made such a rapid recovery.

I speculated that perhaps I might have contracted a bad case of salmonella poisoning from eating raw eggs over several months. I cannot be certain because, as I just noted, the doctors never diagnosed what was wrong with me. All I know is that something had happened that night in the hospital that changed the way I felt. Later I found out that God had spoken to several people to pray for me that specific night. Looking back at it I am convinced that God healed me. Ironically, the twenty plus pounds I had gained over a two-year period of intense exercise had all but disappeared during my sickness. While I gained much of it back over the next couple of years of workouts, the bout with sickness changed my perspective of bodybuilding. It had become somewhat of an idol in my life and I felt God speaking to me and showing me how fleeting it was. I am not knocking exercise and fitness, I am a strong believer in that even today, and I do like to go to the gym regularly, but it is not the center of my life any more. To a degree I felt like Job: the Lord gives and the Lord takes away blessed be the name of the Lord (Job 1:21).

These two examples, I am sure, could be passed off as mere coincidence by some skeptics. And I can appreciate a healthy level of skepticism when it comes to the claim that God "healed" someone of a toe ache or of a pain in a shoulder. While I am not diminishing the way God heals and what type of healing he performs—because nothing is too small for my God (Jer 32:27)—I do know that God is an instantaneous healer and that he continues to do so. Since I started writing this book, God has performed two very real miracles of healing in my family. One in particular is telling of the power of God and the fact that he speaks to his people by this means still today.

The Healer of All Our Diseases

On December 19-20, 2017, my wife and I and our three kids were invited to a resort in West Virginia by my in-laws. Before we had left, my youngest son was running a fever (we thought perhaps due to teething). We prayed for him and he began to show signs of improvement before we left. The same day we arrived at the resort, my daughter became ill with a stomach bug. By the evening she had vomited three times and was not doing well. My wife and I prayed for her and soon she fell asleep. Later that night my wife began to suffer from excruciating dagger-like pains in her stomach. I was not sure what was going on with my family. Was it an attack or were these just natural sicknesses due to a variety of reasons? I knew my wife could take a lot of pain—I had watched her deliver three babies with no medication—so I realized that the pain she was experiencing must be severe if she was unable to move. All the children were in bed by this time except our youngest son, whom my wife was in no shape to tend to. Not only had I been preparing to write this book about God's methods of speaking to his people, but I had also been reading Richard Foster's book *Celebration of Discipline*. In light of these influences, I felt God urging me to pray for my wife with faith believing. I sat on the edge of the bed where my wife was laying and reached over and placed my hand on her stomach. I began to pray just loud enough for her to hear. It was not some super Spirit-infused utterance. As a matter of fact, I was very tired. But I did believe that God was able and that he had heard my prayer. When I finished my prayer my wife quickly fell asleep and slept throughout the night.

When she woke up in the morning she told me that the moment I prayed the pain left her stomach. Did I feel like I had faith above anyone else at that moment? No. But what I did feel is God telling me to pray and to trust him (cf. Matt 17:20; Luke 17:6). God does heal us of all our diseases whether in this life or the next (Ps 103:3). We completed our short vacation feeling fine. Once again I learned a little bit more of how God speaks.

Conclusion

Throughout this chapter I have demonstrated that healings, while perhaps not the normal occurrence every day, are indeed a viable means of God speaking to us if we dare to listen. Although I would love to experience God's healing every time I pray, the reality is

God Speaks through His Acts of Healing

that healings are at the discretion of God. Despite his silence in some situations, I know that God still hears and answers prayer.

Chapter 16

Conclusion

THROUGHOUT THIS BOOK I have attempted to show how God has spoken to me in a personal way in my life. It is through these and many other moments of intimate communication that God has revealed himself to me as a loving Father. But is the only purpose of hearing the voice of God and experiencing his revelation so that a person can be viewed as "super spiritual" or in some way more special than someone else? Those who have experienced such spiritual closeness and revelation of God's will in their lives, I would hope, would humbly reply in the negative. No, the purpose of sharing these experiences is to encourage believers, young and old, that God is real and that he still answers prayers and speaks to people today. This, I am fully aware, is not a logical way to live life especially in a world that scoffs at those who believe in an almighty and living God. Sadly, many today have opted for an existence bathed in post-Enlightenment rationalism as opposed to trusting in the existence of a loving God who still speaks today. Many times those who do experience a true encounter with the God of the universe become objects of ridicule and distrust. But there is something so much more important that I hope my reader has gained from reading the above accounts, namely, a paradigm shift in the way to view God.

Conclusion

A clear biblical example appears in the book of Job. Many people go to the book of Job for the purpose of gaining encouragement in the midst of pain and suffering. While I would never want to deprive a reader from gaining this type of comfort from the book of Job, this is not the only message that resonates from the book. On the contrary, Job is a fine example of how one man moved from a life devoted to his God because of what he had been *taught* or *heard* about God, to a life that had *experienced* God in a real way. The key verse is found in Job 42:5. The passage reads, "By the hearing of the ear, I heard of you, but now my eyes have seen you" (my translation). The old adage, "Seeing is believing." captures the message from the life of Job. Up until his hardships and loss, Job had only *heard* about his God, but when God showed up in the closing chapters of the book and challenged Job with over seventy questions about the greatness of God and his creation, Job's response was one of speechlessness. Indeed, seeing God will do that to the believer (Dan 8:27; Rev 1:17). When one begins to experience the presence of God through his self-revelation by means of dreams, visions, events, prophetic speech, his Word, miracles, healing, and through the encouragement of others, then one's relationship becomes more than one of *hearing* about God, it becomes one of *seeing* and *experiencing* God.

Again, I want to encourage my reader with the reality that until you experience the presence and the revelation of God in your life, you will always be sitting on the proverbial sidelines or on the "bench" in a spiritual sense. Indeed, you may have heard about who God is through your parents, grandparents, a friend or a relative. And you may have heard about all the great things God has done for them and others, but until you experience God for yourself and begin to hear his voice and experience his revelation to you through the events, prayers, and those in your life, you will never truly have that paradigm shift.

For me, having grown up in a Christian home and experiencing God in a "second-hand" fashion for most of my early life, it was not until I learned how God speaks and how he interacts with me in a personal way that I had that paradigm shift for myself.

While I love the way God ministered and spoke to my mother and grandparents in the "good old days" these could only take me so far in my spiritual life. Do not get me wrong, I appreciate my spiritual heritage and would not change it for the world. In fact, that spiritual heritage was the seedbed from which my experience with God took root and sprung forth into the fruit I experience today as a believer. The point I want my readers to take away from this book is simply this, "Taste and see that the Lord is good" (Ps 34:8). When you do this, and when you experience the moving of God and his Spirit in your life, and when you begin to sense his leading and direction through the miraculous, then you will have the paradigm shift that Job experienced. For it is then you can say with confidence, "Before I had heard about God, but now I know God!"

The other main point to consider in light of the previous chapters is the issue of coincidence versus God's intervention and his speaking. What I have attempted to do throughout each chapter is to point out that when you examine a lifetime of "coincidences" you begin to see that these events are more often than not, the moving of God in one's life. They are ways that God has been speaking. I often tell my students that they are in my class for a reason—it is not a "coincidence" that they just happened to choose my class. God has them there so that he can speak to them through lectures and experiences. Indeed, many of my students have told me as much. As I have often repeated, for the believer "coincidences" are in many cases God's intervention. Now that is not to say that every dream, experience, or encounter is of necessity God speaking, but as believers we should be more attuned to the possibilities that God is at work in our lives and even expect it. While many times the Spirit will prompt the believer to the fact that a dream, an experience, or an encounter is from God, sometimes it takes reflection on what has transpired. As I noted in chapter 14, David often reflected on his past experiences (as recorded in 1 and 2 Samuel) and later credited those experiences of blessing, deliverance, or victory to God's intervention in his life as seen in the Psalms.

Conclusion

Therefore, hearing the voice of God takes practice and spiritual alertness. This is nothing to be disheartened about if you have not always recognized God at work in your life. I know I have had to learn, and continue to do so, when God is at work and speaking to me. I am reminded of the two men that Jesus encountered on the road to Emmaus after his resurrection (Luke 24:1–27). These men I am sure knew their Scriptures, yet it took the insight and enlightenment of Jesus for them to recognize that God had been speaking to them and their people for generations through the Law and the Prophets about his coming and his sacrifice.

My prayer is that this book has helped enable the reader to recognize that God is anything but silent in the life of the believer. If we are listening, we will hear him speak. John the Revelator says it well when he records the words of Jesus *to believers*, "Behold, I stand at the door, and knock: if any man hear my voice, and open the door, I will come in to him, and will sup with him, and he with me" (Rev 3:20; KJV). God, not only "knocks," many times he is shouting. Can you hear him speaking to you?

www.ingramcontent.com/pod-product-compliance
Lightning Source LLC
Chambersburg PA
CBHW070505090426
42735CB00012B/2675